ENJOY THE RECIPES

HAPPY COOKING.

Thomas Peterson

Carte du Jour

The Restaurants of Royal Caribbean International

Welcome to *Carte du Jour*, our newest Royal Caribbean International cookbook creation.

The success of our *Savor℠* cookbook series along with the warm response from you, our valued guests, has inspired us to create a cookbook to accompany the launch of our newest ships: *Oasis of the Seas* & *Allure of the Seas*.

This coffee table-style cookbook is unique, as it serves both as a showcase for the wide variety of cooking techniques used onboard, and as a reflection of your cruise experience.

Why the title *Carte du Jour*? The French term is pronounced \kärt-dǝ-'zhur\ and it literally means "card of the day." Translated, this is the *Menu of the Day*. Each chapter of *Carte du Jour* showcases the creativity of Royal Caribbean International's Food & Beverage team and features one of our individual restaurant concepts, focusing on its most popular and successful dishes.

While our main dining rooms remain the core of Royal Caribbean's dining experience, our specialty restaurants continue to enjoy increasing popularity. In the last decade we have expanded our restaurants from *Portofino* on *Voyager of the Seas* to 48 venues fleetwide. Besides the classic favorites of *Portofino* and *Chops Grille*, we have developed exciting new dining options for our guests such as *Giovanni's Table*, a family-style casual Italian venue; *150 Central Park*, which features an exquisite tasting menu and fine-dining experience; *Seafood Shack*, our outdoor, relaxed seafood specialty restaurant; *Izumi*, a Japanese-inspired Asian cuisine and authentic Sushi Bar; and *Solarium Bistro*, introducing a light Spa cuisine in the most spectacular setting at *Oasis of the Seas*.

Our continuous wish to evolve and provide our guests with renewed variety and dining experience has led us to the creation of two new concepts on *Allure of the Seas*: *Rita's Cantina*, a fun and lively Mexican venue and *Samba Grill*, our interpretation of the vibrant lifestyle of Brazil with gauchos serving the best cuts of meat.

While keeping up to date with new trends, most of our new concepts derive from comments and suggestions you, our guests, have made. From conceptional ideas to concept creation, the process takes us through several workshops in our office-based test kitchen at Miami headquarters or onboard our ships. The goal of this fun and creative collaboration between our talented team of Senior Executive Chefs and onboard culinary team members is to provide the most trendy, popular offerings and dining experiences, using only the freshest ingredients available.

Although each dish created goes through a series of critical assessments, the most important ones remain the following:

Are the flavors and textures balanced and varied?

How many steps are involved in the cooking of each dish?

Does the selection appeal to our international clientele?

Will we be able to receive the necessary products onboard consistently?

It is important to add that all our dishes and concepts are tested onboard one of our ship in a controlled environment. During this test phase, the collected feedback and information serve to ensure that, not only do we meet our own high standards, but also the expectations of our guests.

Carte du Jour is a compilation of recipes developed with our guests in mind and will hopefully contain a few of your favorites. Browse through the wide variety of offerings and travel the world from the comfort of your very own kitchen, bringing back memories of your cruise vacation experience onboard Royal Caribbean International.

Bon Voyage and Bon Appétit!

(signature)

Josef Jungwirth
Director, Fleet Culinary Operations

Welcome to *Carte du Jour*, the cookbook that introduces you to the signature dishes found in the specialty restaurants onboard Royal Caribbean International's fleet of ships.

Royal Caribbean is committed to delivering an exceptional onboard dining experience by continuously developing innovative programs and upholding the highest of culinary standards. We strive to constantly deliver new and interesting concepts giving our guests the variety and flexibility to meet their evolving tastes and expectations. Within these pages, we present some of the signature dishes served in nine of our popular onboard specialty restaurants, including those aboard our newest addition in the fleet — the world's largest and most innovative cruise ships, *Oasis of the Seas* and *Allure of the Seas*.

At Royal Caribbean, innovation is in our DNA and that extends to include the many dining options we offer aboard our ships. From breakfast to late night snacks, guests can find an extensive variety of food and beverage offerings that will satisfy any craving or personal preferences. At one of our newest and most contemporary dining venues, *150 Central Park*, guests can savor such dishes as *Sunchoke Cream with Parmesan Froth*, or *Horseradish Crusted Salmon and Sweet Mustard Sauce*. They also can experience a family-style feast influenced by the Tuscan countryside of Italy at *Giovanni's Table*. If guests are looking for something a little lighter, they can sample the fresh and healthful fare at *Solarium Bistro*, or enjoy the *Assorted Sushi Rolls* offered in the Asian bistro, *Izumi*.

While the dishes featured within this book may at first seem daunting to prepare, all recipes are delivered in a simple and straightforward fashion with ingredients and equipment that are readily available. With a tempting selection of dishes, *Carte du Jour* will inspire you to come back to enjoy your Royal Caribbean cruise vacation experience over and over again.

What's more, a portion of the proceeds of your *Carte du Jour* cookbook purchase will benefit *Big Brothers and Big Sisters of Greater Miami*, a volunteer-supported program helping at-risk children succeed through adult mentor relationships.

Thank you for your support and bon appetit!

Adam M. Goldstein

Adam Goldstein
President and CEO
Royal Caribbean International

Big Brothers Big Sisters
of Greater Miami
& Mentoring Resource Center

Big Brothers Big Sisters of Greater Miami is a donor and volunteer supported organization proven to help at-risk children succeed through adult mentor relationships. For information about how you can make a big difference in a young person's life, visit www.wementor.org.

GIOVANNI'S TABLE

DINING ROOM

SOLARIUM

IZUMI

VINTAGES

150 CENTRAL PARK

Table of Contents

SEAFOOD SHACK

CHOPS GRILLE

PORTOFINO

*A*n Italian trattoria with both indoor and al fresco seating featuring Italian classics served family style.

Architectural influences from the landscapes of Tuscany come together to create an atmosphere of casual, relaxed elegance. Vaulted ceilings and alcoves with flickering candles, Italian-style paintings purchased in flea markets combined with street vendors and small vintage shops

Straight out of France and England, enhanced by fresh herbs on the window sill and the subtle aroma of freshly roasted garlic are the trademarks here at Giovanni's.

Giovanni's Tuscan-inspired menu reflects the flavors of the region as well. From the foccaccia per due, freshly sliced prosciutto and Ferrari "affettatrice" (a traditional hand-cranked meat slicer), to the hard Italian cheeses, herbal breads and iced limoncello, you'll think you were dining along the Amalfi coast.

Giovanni's Table

Combine a plate of Lasagna, seasoned by your waiter with a personalized, one-of-a-kind pepper grinder, together with some decadent desserts and Giovani's will bring out the Italian in you. Buonissimo!

Capesante Ai Forno (Oven-baked Crusted Scallops)

ROASTED RED PEPPER PESTO

2 red bell peppers
1 tablespoon (15 ml) extra virgin olive oil
1 ripe tomato, peeled, seeded and chopped
1 clove garlic
2 tablespoons (30 g) pine nuts, toasted
Salt and freshly ground black pepper

½ cup (115 g) slivered almonds, lightly toasted and finely chopped
2 tablespoons (30 g) chopped cilantro
2 tablespoons (30 g) chopped parsley
1 tablespoon (15 g) chopped dill
2 cloves garlic, finely chopped
1 chili pepper, seeds and veins removed, finely chopped
2 teaspoons (10 g) lemon zest
1 cup (235 g) butter, softened
½ teaspoon (2.5 g) salt

BUTTER CRUST

SCALLOPS

24 sea scallops
Salt and freshly ground white pepper
2 tablespoons (30 ml) vegetable oil

GARNISH

1 bunch baby watercress

EQUIPMENT

2 9" x 13" glass or ovenproof baking dishes
2 small glass or stainless steel mixing bowls
Chef's knife and cutting board
Food processor
Large sauté pan or heavy skillet
Serving bowl or small glass bowl

Preheat oven to 400°F or 205°C.

For pesto, place red peppers in an ovenproof dish, drizzle with olive oil and roast for 20 minutes or until brown and blistery. Remove peppers from oven, place them into a small bowl and cover with plastic wrap. A small, tightly closed paper bag will do also. This loosens the skins and eases peeling.

To make crust, in a medium glass or stainless steel bowl, mix all ingredients and transfer to a baking sheet lined with parchment paper. Mold into a roll, cover tightly and refrigerate.

Pat dry scallops and season with salt and pepper. In a large sauté pan over medium heat, warm oil and sear scallops, in batches, for 2 minutes on each side.

Place scallops on a greased ovenproof dish. Slice chilled butter crust mixture and place one slice on top of each scallop.

Bake in the oven for 5 minutes or until butter crust is golden-brown.

Meanwhile, peel roasted peppers and transfer to a food processor, add all remaining ingredients and blend until smooth. Remove to serving bowl.

Arrange scallops on warmed appetizer plates and garnish with a spoonful of pepper pesto and a baby watercress bouquet.

Serves 6.

Difficulty 2.

WINE PAIRING ⌒ FAIRVIEW, CHENIN BLANC, DARLING, SOUTH AFRICA

Sformato di Fontina e Spinaci con Funghi Trifolati e Pomodorini (Double-baked Fontina and Spinach Soufflé)

ONION CONFIT

2 medium onions, peeled and shaved
1/3 cup (90 ml) extra virgin olive oil

SOUFFLÉS

1/2 cup (115 g) unsalted butter
1/2 cup (115 g) all-purpose flour
2 1/2 cups (655 ml) warm milk
1/4 cup (60 g) grated Parmesan cheese
3/4 cup (175 g) shredded Fontina cheese
1 tablespoon (15 g) Dijon mustard
5 eggs, yolk and white separated
4-ounces (120 g) baby spinach, blanched, water squeezed out and chopped
Salt and freshly ground white pepper

PARMESAN GLAZE

1/2 cup (120 ml) heavy cream
1/4 cup (60 g) grated Parmesan cheese
Salt and freshly ground white pepper

VEGETABLE RAGOÛT

1 tablespoon (15 ml) extra virgin olive oil
2 cloves garlic, chopped
4-ounces (120 g) button mushrooms, quartered
1/4 cup (60 ml) dry white wine
1/2 cup (115 g) cherry tomatoes, halved lengthwise
Salt and freshly ground black pepper
1 tablespoon (15 g) chopped parsley

GARNISH

Chive sprigs

EQUIPMENT

1 9" x 13" or larger glass or ovenproof baking dish
2 wire whisks
3 saucepans
6 ramekins or soufflé cups
Chef's knife and cutting board
Large glass or stainless steel bowl
Medium sauté pan
Stand mixer with whisk attachment or large copper or stainless steel mixer
Wooden spoon

Preheat oven to 300°F or 150°C

For confit, in a small saucepan over medium heat, simmer onion in olive oil for 20 minutes. Do not brown. Allow to cool. Cover and reserve.

To make soufflés, in a small saucepan over low heat, melt butter and whisk in flour. Cook roux for 2 minutes (do not brown) then slowly incorporate milk, stirring constantly for 5 to 6 minutes or until smooth and thickened. Remove from heat and allow cooling slightly.

Stir in Parmesan and Fontina cheese. Add Dijon mustard and egg yolk, one at a time, mixing thoroughly. At last fold in chopped spinach and season with salt and pepper.

In a mixing bowl, beat egg whites and a pinch of salt with an electric mixer on medium speed until eggs are frothy. Increase speed to high and beat until they form soft peaks.

Spoon one-third of egg whites in cheese mixture and gently mix until the batter is lightened. Fold in remaining egg whites, taking care not to deflate them. Divide mixture into greased individual molds set in a shallow pan or baking dish. Pour water into the pan until it is halfway up the sides of the molds and bake for 20 to 25 minutes or until soufflés have risen and are lightly colored. Remove from heat and allow cooling.

In a small saucepan over medium heat, bring heavy cream to a boil. Remove from heat and whisk in cheese. Season to taste and keep warm.

For ragoût, in a sauté pan over medium heat, warm oil and sauté garlic for 2 minutes. Add mushrooms and sauté for 2 to 3 minutes. Deglaze with wine and add tomatoes. Season with salt and pepper and simmer until all liquid has evaporated. Stir in parsley at the last minute.

Just before serving, remove soufflés from molds and reheat for 5 to 7 minutes or until the soufflés rise again. Delicately center each soufflé on a warmed plate. Coat with Parmesan glaze and surround with vegetable ragoût. Garnish with chive sprigs.

Serves 6.

Difficulty 4.

Insalata alla Cesare (Caesar Salad)

INGREDIENTS

3/4 pound (375 g) radicchio, sliced
3/4 pound (375 g) romaine, sliced
1/4 cup (60 g) Parmesan cheese, shaved

CROUTONS

1 cup (250 g) cubed sourdough bread
4 tablespoons (60 ml) extra virgin olive oil
Salt and freshly ground black pepper

DRESSING

3 cloves garlic
3 tablespoons (45 ml) freshly squeezed lemon
juice
5 anchovy fillets, drained or
2 teaspoons (10 g) anchovy paste
2 teaspoons (10 g) Dijon mustard
2 teaspoons (10 ml) Worcestershire sauce
2 egg yolks
1 cup (240 ml) extra virgin olive oil
Salt

EQUIPMENT

Blender or food processor
Chef's knife and cutting board
Small glass or stainless steel bowl
Standard baking sheet

Preheat oven to 380°F or 195°C.

To prepare croutons, place bread on a baking sheet and drizzle with olive oil. Toss well to coat evenly. Season to taste with salt and black pepper. Bake for 10 minutes or until crisp and golden brown. Rotate to ensure even browning. Set aside to cool on a paper towel.

To prepare Caesar dressing, combine all ingredients except oil in a blender or food processor. Blend until smooth. While processing, slowly add oil. Adjust seasoning, transfer in a small glass or stainless steel bowl, cover and refrigerate.

Place radicchio and romaine lettuces on chilled plates, drizzle with Caesar dressing, and garnish with Parmesan shavings and croutons.

Serve immediately.

Serves 6.

Difficulty 1.

WINE PAIRING ✒ MANDRAROSSA, NERO D' AVOLA, SICILIA, ITALY

Focaccie alla Giovanni (Italian Flat Bread Giovanni's Style)

DOUGH

2 tablespoons (30 g) yeast
1/4 cup (60 ml) hot water
4 cups (920 g) all-purpose flour, sifted
1 tablespoon (15 g) salt
2 tablespoons (30 ml) extra virgin olive oil
1 3/4 cups (420 ml) water, room temperature

1/4 cup (60 ml) extra virgin
olive oil for drizzling

TOMATO SAUCE

2 tablespoons (30 ml) extra virgin olive oil
1 yellow onion, chopped
2 cloves garlic, chopped
1 tablespoon (15 g) tomato paste
2 pounds (900 g) fresh tomatoes,
peeled, seeded and diced
1/2 teaspoon (2.5 g) granulated sugar
Salt and freshly ground black pepper
1/4 bunch fresh basil, julienned

GARNISH

2 cups (465 g) shredded mozzarella cheese
1/4 bunch basil, julienned

EQUIPMENT

1 small glass bowl
1 large glass or stainless steel bowl
2 standard baking sheets
4 medium glass or stainless steel bowls
1 12" x 18" (30 cm x 45 cm) baking pan
Chef's knife and cutting board
Medium saucepan
Pastry rack or cooling rack
Wooden spoon

Preheat oven to 420°F or 215°C.

For dough, dissolve yeast and hot water in a small glass bowl. Let sit for 2 minutes or until water is cloudy. Place flour and salt in a large glass or stainless steel bowl. Pour in yeast mixture and remaining ingredients and, using a fork, mix thoroughly until dough forms a ball.

Divide into 4 equal pieces and place each dough into a separate oiled bowl. Cover each bowl with plastic wrap and let rest for 1 hour at room temperature.

Transfer dough into an oiled baking pan and spread very gently with oiled fingers until desired thickness, about 1 1/2-inch or 4 cm thick. Repeat with remaining dough.

Drizzle with olive oil and, using your fingers, gently imprint holes in the dough surface; this increases the surface area of the dough and aids in even baking. Let rest for 1 hour.

Meanwhile, prepare the tomato sauce by warming the oil in a saucepan over medium heat. Add onions and sauté for 5 minutes or until translucent. Add garlic, tomato paste, fresh tomatoes and sugar. Season with salt and pepper, bring to a boil and simmer for 20 minutes or until tomatoes are fully cooked and sauce has thickened. Stir in basil at the last minute.

Drizzle the surface of each dough with more oil, spread with tomato sauce and liberally sprinkle with shredded cheese. Finish with fresh julienned basil.

Bake for 25 minutes and allow to cool for a couple minutes before slicing.

You can customize your bread in many ways – try different toppings such as oregano, sliced tomatoes, sautéed potatoes, Parma ham…

You can also add ingredients to the dough. Once the dry ingredients are incorporated add items such as sliced kalamata olives, fresh herbs, chopped walnuts…

Makes 4 pieces.
Difficulty 2.

Lasagna Tradizionale al Sugo di Carne (Traditional Meat Lasagna)

LASAGNA

Sea salt
1 tablespoon (15 ml) vegetable oil
1 26-ounce (454 g) package lasagna pasta
   or pasta sheets, store bought
4-ounces (120 g) grated Parmesan cheese
4-ounces (120 g) shredded Monterey cheese

MEAT SAUCE

1 tablespoon (15 ml) extra virgin olive oil
2 medium yellow onions, diced
2 cloves garlic, diced
1 pound (450 g) lean ground beef or turkey
1 tablespoon (15 g) tomato paste
1/4 cup (60 ml) red wine
1 (16-ounce) or (450 g) can of chopped tomato
1 cup (240 ml) water
1/2 teaspoon (2.5 g) sugar
2 tablespoons (30 g) Herbes de Provence
   or Italian seasoning blend
Salt and freshly ground black pepper

WHITE SAUCE

1/3 cup (85 g) butter
1/3 cup (85 g) all-purpose flour
1 teaspoon (5 g) ground nutmeg
1 teaspoon (5 g) salt
2 cups (475 ml) warm milk

GARNISH

Julienne basil

EQUIPMENT

1 9" x 13" (23 x 33 cm) glass
   or ovenproof baking dish
Cheese grater
Chef's knife and cutting board
Large pot or stockpot
Large saucepan
Small saucepan
Rubber spatula
Wire whisk
Wooden spoon

Preheat oven to 350°F or 175°C.

To soften lasagna, bring a large pot of salted water and oil to a boil. Add pasta 2 to 3 at a time and stir. Return to a boil and cook for 5 minutes or until lasagna sheets are soft. Remove from water and lay on wax paper or aluminum foil to avoid stickiness.

For meat sauce, in a saucepan over medium heat, warm oil and sauté onions for 5 minutes or until translucent. Add garlic and sauté for 2 minutes. Add meat and cook for 6 to 8 minutes or until meat begins to brown. Stir in tomato paste and deglaze with wine. Add chopped tomatoes, water, sugar and herbs and mix well. Season with salt and pepper, cover and simmer for 30 minutes.

For white sauce, in a small saucepan over low heat, melt butter and whisk in flour, nutmeg and salt. Cook roux for 2 minutes (do not brown) then slowly incorporate milk, stirring constantly for 5 to 6 minutes or until smooth and thickened.

Mix cheeses in a small glass or stainless steel bowl.

To build lasagna, pour 2 to 3 tablespoons of meat sauce in a 9"x13" pan, top with a layer of pasta (lengthwise), a layer of white sauce, a layer of meat sauce and sprinkle with cheese mix. Repeat twice ending with cheese.

Bake for 30 minutes and serve in warmed plates, garnished with julienned basil. Enjoy with your favorite Chianti.

Serves 6.

Difficulty 3.

WINE PAIRING ⌒ MICHELE CHIARLO, BARBERA D' ASTI, "LE ORME" SUPERIORE, ITALY

WINE PAIRING ❧ DANZANTE, PINOT GRIGIO, VENEZIE, ITALY

Tonno con Olive e Patate

(Pepper-crusted Tuna Fillet Atop a Potato-olive Ragoût)

RAGOÛT

2 tablespoons (30 ml) extra virgin olive oil
1 yellow onion, diced
1 clove garlic, chopped
6 medium new potatoes, peeled and diced
2 plum tomatoes, peeled, seeded and diced
½ red bell pepper, cut in small cubes
2 cups (475 ml) chicken stock (page 172)
1 cup (240 ml) clam juice
Salt and freshly ground black pepper
¼ cup (60 g) pitted kalamata olives, sliced
1 teaspoon (5 g) basil pesto, purchased
1 teaspoon (15 g) chopped parsley

TUNA

6 (6-ounce) or (170 g) fresh ahi tuna steaks
3 tablespoons (45 g) mixed peppercorn, coarsely cracked
1 tablespoon (15 ml) extra virgin olive oil

PESTO OIL

2 tablespoons (30 g) basil pesto, purchased
¼ cup (60 ml) extra virgin olive oil

GARNISH

Basil sprigs

EQUIPMENT

Cast-iron skillet or heavy-bottom frying pan
Chef's knife and cutting board
Non-stick skillet
Parchment paper
Small glass bowl
Wooden spoon

To make ragoût, in a heavy bottom skillet over medium heat, warm oil and sauté onion and garlic for 5 minutes or until lightly colored. Add potatoes and fry for 8 minutes. Add tomatoes and peppers, and moisten with half of the chicken stock and clam juice. Season with salt and pepper and simmer for 30 minutes or until potatoes are tender to the touch, adding remaining stock and clam juice as necessary. At the last minute, gently incorporate olives, pesto and parsley.

For tuna, spread cracked pepper on a parchment paper and firmly press tuna fillets onto them on all sides. In a non-stick skillet over medium-high heat, warm oil and cook tuna fillets on all sides for 8 minutes for medium-rare tuna. Remove from heat and slice crosswise.

Mix pesto and olive oil in a small glass bowl. Delicately arrange tuna atop a heap of potato ragoût. Drizzle with pesto oil and garnish with basil sprigs.

Serves 6.

Difficulty 2.

Bellini

1 fresh peach, peeled, pitted and quartered or ¼ cup frozen peaches, thawed
¼ teaspoon (1 g) grated orange zest
2 oz. (6 cl) simple syrup (page 173)
3 oz. (9 cl) Prosecco or sparkling wine

Place first 3 ingredients in a blender and purée until smooth. Pour 2 tablespoons of peach mixture into a Champagne flute and slowly top off with Prosecco. Stir to blend and garnish with a peach sliver.

Wild Blossom Martini

1 ¼ oz. (3.75 cl) gin
¾ oz. (2.25 cl) St. Germain Elderflower liqueur
¼ oz. (0.75 cl) Amaretto Disaronno Originale
¼ oz. (0.75 cl) Patrón Citronge orange liqueur
1 oz. (3 cl) Sweet & Sour mix

Combine all ingredients in a cocktail shaker with ice. Shake and strain into a chilled martini glass. Garnish with a lemon twist.

Giovanni's Table

Ossobuco alla Piemontese (Veal Ossobuco Au Jus)

VEAL SHANKS

2 tablespoons (30 ml) extra virgin olive oil
6 12-ounce to 1 pound
(340 to 375 g) veal shank
2 yellow onions, small diced
2 carrots, small diced
2 celery stalks, small diced
2 cloves garlic, peeled and diced
1 cup (240 ml) dry white wine
1 15-ounce (450 g) can diced tomatoes
3 cups (710 ml) veal demi-glace (page 173)
Salt and freshly ground black pepper

MUSHROOMS

1 tablespoon (15 ml) extra virgin olive oil
1 clove garlic, minced
5-ounce (140 g) button mushrooms, quartered
3-ounce (85 g) cherry tomatoes, quartered
Salt and freshly ground black pepper

BEANS

2 tablespoons (30 g) butter
8-ounces (230 g) green beans,
blanched and refreshed in ice water
Salt

POLENTA

1 1/2 quarts (1.4 L) water
2 teaspoons (10 g) salt
1 3/4 cups (410 g) yellow cornmeal
3 tablespoons (45 g) butter
1/4 cup (60 g) grated Parmesan

GARNISH

Rosemary sprigs

EQUIPMENT

Cheesecloth
Chef's knife and cutting board
Heavy pot or Dutch oven
Large saucepan
Large sauté pan
Metal tongs
Small sauté pan
Wooden spoon
Wire whisk

Preheat oven to 375°F or 190°C.

Season veal shanks with salt and pepper. Heat a Dutch oven or heavy stockpot over medium-high heat for 2 minutes. Warm oil and sear veal shanks in batches, turning occasionally, until they are well browned on all sides, about 8 minutes. Remove shanks and set aside.

Into the same Dutch oven, add onions, carrots, celery and garlic and sauté for 5 minutes. Deglaze with wine, add tomatoes and veal stock and bring to a boil. Return shanks to Dutch oven, making sure that they are covered in liquid. Cover and cook in the oven for 1 1/2 hours, turning occasionally, until meat is falling off the bone.

Remove shanks from pot and keep warm. Strain liquid through a cheesecloth. Skim off all the fat that rises to the surface of the jus. Season with salt and pepper to taste.

In a small sauté pan over medium heat, warm oil and sauté garlic for 2 minutes. Add mushrooms and tomatoes and sauté for 3 minutes. Stir in 1/2 cup (120 ml) of the jus and simmer for 10 minutes or until mushrooms are cooked through. Season with salt and pepper and keep warm.

Simmer the remaining jus for 10 minutes or until it has reduced by half.

Make polenta by bringing a heavy saucepan of salted water to a boil over high heat and gradually whisking in cornmeal. Reduce heat to low and cook, stirring often for about 15 minutes or until mixture thickens and cornmeal is tender. Add butter and Parmesan cheese. Taste and rectify seasoning as needed.

For green beans, in a large sauté pan over medium heat, melt butter and sauté for 3 minutes, or until warm. Season with salt.

Arrange polenta off-center on warmed plates, top with green beans and veal shank. Spoon mushroom mixture around ossobuco and garnish with a rosemary sprig. Finish off with a drizzle of au jus.

Serves 6.

Difficulty 5.

WINE PAIRING ~ SPY VALLEY, PINOT NOIR, MARLBOROUGH, NEW ZEALAND

Giovanni's Table

WINE PAIRING ✑ RAVENSWOOD, "OLD VINE" ZINFANDEL, SONOMA, CALIFORNIA

Scaloppine di Vitello al Granchio

(Veal Scaloppine with Basil Hollandaise)

ONION CONFIT

1/2 head of garlic, peeled and shaved
2 medium onions, peeled and shaved
1/3 cup (90 ml) extra virgin olive oil

MASHED POTATOES

2 pounds (900 g) Yukon Gold potatoes, peeled and quartered
3/4 cup (175 ml) heavy cream
2 tablespoons (30 g) unsalted butter
Salt and freshly ground white pepper

BASIL HOLLANDAISE

1 pound (450 g) butter
1/4 bunch basil leaves
2 shallots, peeled and finely chopped
3 tablespoons (45 ml) dry white wine
3 tablespoons (45 ml) white wine vinegar
15 black peppercorns, crushed
6 egg yolks
Juice of half lemon
Salt

CRAB

6-ounces (180 g) crab meat
3 tablespoons (45 ml) dry white wine
1/3 cup (85 g) heavy cream
Salt and freshly ground white pepper

VEAL SCALOPPINE

12 veal scaloppine, 1 1/2 to 2-inches (4 cm) thick
Salt and freshly ground black pepper
2 tablespoons (30 ml) dry white wine
1/3 cup (90 ml) veal demi-glace (page 173)

ASPARAGUS

12 green asparagus, peeled, blanched and refreshed in ice water
Salt and freshly ground white pepper

EQUIPMENT

4 saucepans
Chef's knife and cutting board
Fine sieve
Glass or stainless steel bowls
Large pot or stockpot
Large skillet
Potato ricer
Small sauté pan
Tongs
Wooden spoon
Wire whisk

For the onion confit, in a small saucepan over medium heat, simmer garlic and onions in olive oil for 20 minutes. Do not brown. Allow to cool. Cover and reserve.

For mashed potatoes, place potatoes into salted cold water, bring to a boil and cook until potatoes are easily pierced with the tip of a knife, about 15 minutes. Drain and press potatoes through a potato ricer into a heated bowl. Stir in cream and butter. Adjust seasoning with salt and pepper. Set aside and keep warm.

To make hollandaise, in a small saucepan over low heat, combine butter and basil and gently simmer for 5 minutes. Do not brown. Discard basil leaves and skim the surface of the butter fat to remove the foam. Remove the clear butter fat into a second saucepan. Discard the milky liquid (whey) at the bottom of the pan. Keep butter fat warm.

In a small saucepan over medium heat, combine shallots, white wine, vinegar and peppercorns and cook for 3 minutes stirring constantly. Strain liquid through a fine

sieve into a medium glass or non reactive bowl and place over a pan filled with simmering water. Add egg yolks and gently cook, whisking constantly for 8 to 10 minutes or until mixture becomes frothy and pale in color. Stir in lemon juice and salt.

Remove from heat and slowly incorporate clarified butter, in one continuous stream, whisking constantly for about 10 minutes or until the sauce thickens and acquires the consistency of a mayonnaise. Strain through a fine sieve into a clean, warmed glass bowl and adjust seasoning. Keep warm in bain-marie.

For crab, in a small sauté pan over medium heat, warm 2 tablespoons (30 ml) onion confit and sauté crab meat for 3 minutes. Deglaze with white wine and add heavy cream. Season with salt and pepper, reduce heat to low and simmer for 8 minutes or until thickened. Stir in 4 tablespoons (60 ml) basil hollandaise and keep warm.

For veal, season scaloppine with salt and pepper. Heat 2 tablespoons (30 ml) onion confit in a large skillet

over medium heat and sauté veal for 3 minutes on each side. Work in batches if necessary and transfer veal to a warmed platter. Cover and keep warm. Deglaze the skillet with white wine and add veal demi-glace. Simmer for 2 minutes.

Reheat asparagus by plunging them in boiling water for 2 minutes. Drain well and sauté with warmed onion confit in a small saucepan over medium heat for 2 minutes. Season all vegetables with salt and pepper.

Arrange mashed potatoes in the center of warmed plates. Top with a slice of veal, a spoonful of crab, a couple asparagus stalks and a second slice of veal. Drizzle with basil hollandaise and garnish with chopped chives and basil sprigs.

Finish with a spoonful of veal demi-glace.

Serves 6.

Difficulty 5.

Bomboloni alla Toscana

(Tuscan Doughnuts with Warm Chocolate Sauce)

BOMBOLONI
1 tablespoon (15 g) dry yeast
2 tablespoons (30 ml) lukewarm water
3 1/2 cups (815 g) all-purpose flour
4 eggs
1/3 cup (85 g) granulated sugar
1 teaspoon (5 g) salt
1/4 cup (60 ml) milk
3/4 cup (175 g) unsalted butter, cubed
Vegetable oil for frying

CUSTARD
1 cup (240 ml) milk
1 vanilla bean, split
4 egg yolks
1/3 cup (85 g) granulated sugar
1/4 cup (60 g) all-purpose flour, sifted

GARNISH
1/4 cup (60 g) granulated sugar
1/2 cup (120 ml) chocolate sauce, purchased, warmed
Mint sprigs

EQUIPMENT
1 large glass or stainless steel bowl
2 small glass or stainless steel bowls
2 small, heavy saucepans
Chef's knife and cutting board
Large, heavy-bottom saucepan (or deep fryer)
Pastry bag with medium, round tip
Rubber spatula and wire whisk
Stand mixer with paddle attachment (or hand-held mixer)
Slotted spoon
Standard baking sheet

To make bomboloni, place yeast and water into a small bowl and mix until yeast has dissolved.

Place flour, eggs, sugar and salt in a stand mixer fitted with the paddle attachment and beat at medium speed for 10 seconds. Add yeast mixture and milk and beat for 3 minutes at medium-high speed or until dough holds together. Add cubed butter and beat for another 5 minutes or until dough no longer sticks to the side of the mixing bowl.

Remove dough from mixing bowl, spread over a lightly floured baking sheet and flatten until it is about 3/4-inch thick. Cover with plastic wrap and refrigerate for 2 hours.

Meanwhile, for custard, combine milk and vanilla bean in a saucepan, over medium heat and bring to a boil.

In a glass or stainless steel bowl, whisk together egg yolks and sugar for 5 minutes or until mixture has thickened, add flour and mix well. Discard vanilla pod and incorporate hot milk into egg mixture a little at a time, whisking constantly.

Transfer mixture back into the saucepan and slowly cook over low heat for about 10 minutes or until mixture pulls from the sides of the saucepan. Do not boil. Stir often. Remove from heat and allow to cool.

To finish bomboloni, transfer dough to a lightly floured surface and cut into circles using a 1 1/2-inch (3.8 cm) round cookie cutter.

Place disks on a baking sheet covered with greased parchment paper. Cover with plastic wrap and allow to proof, at room temperature, for 2 hours.

Fry doughnuts, in batches, in hot oil (320°F or 160°C) for 5 to 7 minutes or until golden brown.

Using a slotted spoon, transfer doughnuts on a baking sheet lined with paper towels.

Fill the center of each mini doughnut with custard by using a pastry bag fitted with a medium tip, and roll into granulated sugar.

Serve warmed bombolonis on dessert plates with a side dish of chocolate sauce.

Serves 6.
Difficulty 2.

WINE PAIRING ⌐ FAIRVIEW, CHENIN BLANC, DARLING, SOUTH AFRICA

Josef Jungwirth, Director, Culinary Operations

WITH 10,000 CRYSTAL ELEMENTS, A HEIGHT OF 18 FEET (5.50 METERS), A DIAMETER OF 10.5 FEET (3.20 METERS), AND A WEIGHT OF 2,095 POUNDS (950 KG), THE MAIN CHANDELIER SETS THE TONE WITH AN ELEGANT, EXPANSIVE GRANDEUR, A GILDED DESIGN AND AN ART DECO TOUCH.

THE MAIN MURAL, WHICH WAS FIRST MAPPED OUT IN DETAIL IN SMALL-SCALE PAINTINGS, WAS LATER PAINTED IN 3 SEGMENTS, EACH TAKING APPROXIMATELY 2 MONTHS TO COMPLETE, FEATURING A CENTER FIGURE OVER 9 FEET TALL.

SHARE A CLASSIC MEAL WITH FAMILY OR FRIENDS. EACH DISH IS PREPARED WITH OUR TALENTED CHEFS' OWN SPECIAL TWISTS. CHOOSE A WINE FROM OUR EXTENSIVE WINE LIST AND ALLOW US TO PAMPER YOU.

Dining Room

THE DINING ROOMS ONBOARD ROYAL CARIBBEAN INTERNATIONAL BRING TO MIND AN EARLIER TIME, WHEN TRANSATLANTIC CROSSINGS WERE THE CIVILIZED WAY TO JOURNEY BETWEEN CONTINENTS. WE HAVE UPDATED THE EXPERIENCE WITH ALL THE CONVENIENCES OF THIS CENTURY, SUCH AS "MY TIME DINING", ALLOWING YOU, OUR GUESTS, THE FLEXIBILITY TO DINE AT YOUR LEISURE THROUGHOUT YOUR VOYAGE.

Citrus Seafood Salad

MARINADE

1/3 cup (45 ml) rice vinegar
Juice of 2 lemons
2 tablespoons (30 g) granulated sugar

SALAD

12 medium size shrimp, peeled, deveined and
tail on
6 sea scallops
6 slices smoked salmon

VINAIGRETTE

1/4 cup (60 ml) rice vinegar
1 tablespoon (15 ml) light soy sauce
Juice of 1 lime
Salt and freshly ground black pepper
3 tablespoons (45 ml) vegetable oil

GARNISH

2 Lebanese cucumbers, seeded and thinly sliced
3-ounces (85 g) daikon sprouts
Chive sprigs
2 lemons, quartered
Sesame seeds

EQUIPMENT

1 small glass baking dish
2 small glass or stainless steel bowls
Chef's knife and cutting board
Wire whisk

To make marinade, in a small stainless steel bowl, combine all ingredients. Place shrimp and scallops in a shallow dish and coat with marinade. Cover and refrigerate for 3 hours.

For vinaigrette, in a stainless steel or glass bowl, combine first 4 ingredients. Slowly whisk in oil until blended.

Arrange marinated seafood and smoked salmon on chilled plates. Garnish with cucumber slice, daikon sprouts, chive sprigs and lemon. Drizzle with rice vinaigrette and sprinkle with sesame seeds.

Serves 6.

Difficulty 1.

Hot and Sour Prawn Soup

SOUP

1 quart (1 L) chicken stock (page 172)
1 1/2 tablespoons (23 g) Tom Yum
  paste, purchased
2 lemongrass stalks, halved lengthwise
4 Kaffir lime leaves
1/4 teaspoon (1 g) Thai
  shrimp paste, purchased
1 tablespoon (15 ml) fish sauce
1 teaspoon (5 g) granulated sugar, if necessary
1 chili pepper, seeded and chopped
  Juice of 1 lime
1 (7.4-ounce) (210 g) can peeled large straw
  mushrooms, halved
18 prawns, raw, peeled and
  deveined (size 31/40)
1/4 bunch coriander leaves

GARNISH

Coriander sprigs

EQUIPMENT

2 large pots or stockpots
Chef's knife and cutting board
Fine mesh strainer or Chinois
Ladle
Wooden spoon

To make soup, in a large stockpot over medium heat, warm chicken stock and whisk in Tom Yum paste.

Stir in lemongrass, Kaffir lime leaves and shrimp paste and bring to a boil. Simmer for 10 to 15 minutes or until broth has reduced by 1/4. Add fish sauce and taste broth. Add the sugar a little at a time should the soup taste too sour to your pallet. Add chili as needed, based on the spiciness desired.

Strain broth into a clean stockpot and stir in lime juice, straw mushrooms, prawns and coriander. Simmer for 5 to 7 minutes or until mushrooms are hot and prawns are cooked through.

Ladle soup into warmed bowls, equally dividing the mushrooms and prawns and garnish with coriander sprigs.

Serves 6.

Difficulty 1.

Luxury Martini

2 oz. (6 cl) vodka or gin
1/4 oz. (0.75 cl) dry vermouth

Fill shaker with ice and add all ingredients. Shake well and strain into a chilled martini glass. Garnish with a lemon twist or pitted green olives.

Pan-fried Cauliflower Cakes

GARLIC CONFIT

1 head of garlic, peeled and shaved
1/3 cup (90 ml) extra virgin olive oil

PANCAKES

1/2 cup (115 g) flour
1 teaspoon (5 g) baking powder
1 egg
2 tablespoons (30 ml) extra virgin olive oil
1/3 cup (90 ml) milk
Salt and freshly ground black pepper
1 head cauliflower, cored,
  steamed and coarsely chopped
1 tablespoon (15 g) finely chopped parsley

VEGETABLES

2 red bell peppers, sliced
2 medium tomatoes, peeled, seeded and julienned
Salt and freshly ground black pepper
1 tablespoon (15 g) chopped parsley

ASPARAGUS

2 tablespoons (30 ml) garlic confit
18 asparagus, blanched
Salt and freshly ground black pepper

CREAM

1/2 cup (120 ml) sour cream
2 tablespoons (30 g) chopped cilantro

GARNISH

1 small white onion, thinly sliced into rings,
  dusted with flour and deep-fried
Parsley sprigs

EQUIPMENT

1 griddle pan or large sauté pan
1 large glass or stainless steel bowl
1 medium sauté pan
1 small glass or stainless steel bowl
1 small saucepan
Chef's knife and cutting board
Ladle
Wire whisk

Preheat oven to 350°F or 175°C.

In a small saucepan over medium heat, simmer garlic in olive oil for 20 minutes. Do not brown. Allow to cool. Cover and reserve.

To make batter, place sifted flour in a stainless steel bowl, add baking powder, egg and olive oil and mix well. Add milk a little at the time. Season with salt and pepper. Cover and let rest for 1/2 hour.

In a sauté pan over medium heat, warm 3 tablespoons (45 ml) garlic confit, add peppers and sauté for 3 minutes. Add tomatoes and sauté for another 3 minutes. Season with salt and pepper and finish with chopped parsley.

Meanwhile warm a griddle at medium heat and grease thoroughly.

Fold cauliflower and parsley into pancake batter.

Using a small ladle pour batter on griddle, forming 4-inches (10 cm) diameter pancakes and cook for 3 minutes on each side, turning once. Drain and place on a sheet pan lined with paper towels. Keep warm in the oven, leaving the door open.

In a sauté pan over medium heat, warm garlic confit and sauté asparagus for 2 minutes or until heated through. Season with salt and pepper. Keep warm.

For cream, mix all ingredients in a small glass or stainless steel bowl.

To plate, stack 2 cauliflower pancakes and top with asparagus and pepper mixture. Finish with onion rings and parsley sprigs. Serve cilantro cream on the side.

Serves 6.
Difficulty 1.

WINE PAIRING ∽ MACMURRAY RANCH, PINOT GRIS, SONOMA COAST, CALIFORNIA

WINE PAIRING ∽ SAUVIGNON BLANC, MONTGRAS, CENTRAL VALLEY, CHILE

Golden Sea Bass
with Spanish Sofrito and Olive Polenta

ONION CONFIT

1/2 head of garlic, peeled and shaved
2 medium onions, peeled and shaved
1/3 cup (90 ml) extra virgin olive oil

SPANISH SOFRITO

1 tablespoon (15 ml) extra virgin olive oil
1 tablespoon (15 ml) onion confit
1 yellow onion, diced
1 clove garlic, minced
1 red bell pepper, diced
1 yellow bell pepper, diced
1 green bell pepper, diced
2 tablespoons (30 ml) dry white wine
1/4 cup (60 ml) chicken stock (page 172)
Salt and freshly ground black pepper
1 teaspoon (5 g) chopped parsley

POLENTA

1 1/2 quarts (1.4 L) water
2 teaspoons (10 g) salt
1 3/4 cups (410 g) yellow cornmeal
3 tablespoons (45 g) butter
1/4 cup (60 g) grated Parmesan
1-ounce (30 g) pitted black olives, diced

BABY CARROTS

12 baby carrots, peeled and blanched
1 tablespoon (15 ml) onion confit

FISH

6 (7-ounce) (200 g) sea bass fillets
2 tablespoons (30 ml) extra virgin olive oil
Salt and freshly ground white pepper

WILTED SPINACH

2 tablespoons (30 ml) onion confit
1/2 pound (250 g) fresh spinach, stems off
Salt and freshly ground black pepper

GARNISH

1 small white onion, thinly sliced into rings,
dusted with flour and deep-fried

EQUIPMENT

2 small saucepans
3 large sauté pans
Chef's knife and cutting board
Heavy saucepan or small stockpot
Wooden spoon

Preheat oven to 350°F or 175°C.

For the onion confit, in a small saucepan over medium heat, simmer garlic and onion in olive oil for 20 minutes. Do not brown. Allow to cool. Cover and reserve.

To make sofrito, in a sauté pan over medium heat, warm olive oil and onion confit and sauté onion and garlic for 4 minutes or until onions are translucent. Toss in peppers and sauté for 5 minutes. Deglaze with wine, add chicken stock and simmer for 10 minutes or until peppers are soft. Season with salt and pepper, stir in chopped parsley and keep warm.

Make polenta by bringing a heavy saucepan of salted water to a boil over high heat and gradually whisking in cornmeal. Reduce heat to low and cook, stirring often for

about 15 minutes or until mixture thickens and cornmeal is tender. Add butter, Parmesan cheese and olives. Taste and rectify seasoning as needed.

Season fish with salt and pepper. In a sauté pan over high heat, warm oil and sear fish for 1 minute on each side. Arrange on a sheet pan and finish in the oven for 5 to 7 minutes.

Reheat carrots by dipping them into boiling water for 2 to 3 minutes or until heated through. In a small saucepan over medium heat, warm onion confit and sauté carrots for 1 minute.

For spinach, in a sauté pan over medium heat, warm confit and sauté spinach for 2 minutes. Season with salt and pepper. Drain excess water.

Serve a piece of fried onion-garnished sea bass atop a spoonful of polenta in the center of warmed plates and finish with Spanish sofrito, some wilted spinach and a couple of baby carrots.

Serves 6.

Difficulty 2.

Mediterranean Seafood Medley

COMPOTE

1/4 cup (60 ml) extra virgin olive oil
4 cloves garlic, julienned
1 (28-ounce) (794 g) can whole tomatoes, drained and cut into stripes
1/4 bunch fresh basil, julienned
1 large eggplant, cut into large cubes
Salt and freshly ground black pepper

SABAYON

1/4 cup frozen sweet corn kernels
3 egg yolks
1/2 cup (120 ml) dry white wine
1/2 cup (120 ml) white vinegar

SEAFOOD

6 (4-ounce) (120 g) monkfish fillets
6 medium size shrimp, peeled, deveined and tail on (16/20)
6 sea scallops
Sea salt and freshly ground black pepper
2 tablespoons (30 ml) extra virgin olive oil

VEGETABLES

2 tablespoons (30 g) butter
1 small yellow onion, diced
1 cup (235 g) frozen sweet peas, steamed
1 cup (235 g) frozen sweet corn, steamed
1/2 cup (115 g) grape tomatoes, halved
1 teaspoon (5 g) sea salt & freshly ground black pepper

BALSAMIC REDUCTION

1/4 cup (60 ml) balsamic vinegar
(reduced by 2/3 over medium heat)

GARNISH

Thyme sprigs

EQUIPMENT

1 small saucepan
2 medium saucepans
Blender or immersion blender
Chef's knife and cutting board
Fine mesh strainer or Chinois
Medium glass or stainless steel bowl
Pastry rings or ramekins
Standard baking sheet

Preheat oven to 320°F or 160°C.

To make compote, in a saucepan over medium heat, warm 2 tablespoons (30 ml) of oil and sauté garlic for 3 minutes. Add tomatoes and simmer for 15 minutes or until all liquid is absorbed. Season with salt and pepper and add julienned basil. Keep warm.

Meanwhile, in a sauté pan over medium heat, warm remaining oil and sauté eggplant for 10 minutes or until cooked through. Season with salt and pepper and fold into tomato mixture. Keep warm on the side of the stove.

For sabayon, place corn in a blender and blend to a puréed consistency. Pass through a fine sieve.

In a medium size glass bowl over bain-marie (bowl over simmering water) whisk egg yolks with corn mixture until foamy. Incorporate wine and vinegar a little at a time, whisking constantly for 10 minutes. Remove from heat and keep warm.

Pat dry fish and seafood and season with salt and pepper. In a sauté pan over high heat, warm oil and sear fish and seafood for 1 minute on each side working in batches if necessary. Arrange on a sheet pan and finish in the oven for 5 to 7 minutes.

For vegetables, in a sauté pan over medium heat, melt butter and sauté onion for 4 minutes or until translucent. Toss in peas, corn and tomatoes and sauté for 3 minutes or until vegetables are warmed through. Season with salt and pepper and keep warm.

Fill in small pastry rings or ramekins with eggplant mixture and transfer onto warmed plates. Gently remove pastry ring (or up-turned ramekin) and lean fish and seafood against eggplant. Surround with vegetables and finish with drizzles of corn sabayon and Balsamic reduction.

Garnish with fresh thyme sprigs.

Serves 6.

Difficulty 5.

Wine Pairing ⌘ Château La Nerthe, Blanc, Châteauneuf-du-Pape, France

WINE PAIRING ⸺ CHATEAU STE. MICHELLE, DRY ROSÉ, "NELLIE'S GARDEN", COLUMBIA VALLEY, WASHINGTON

Chicken Yakitory

MARINADE

1/3 cup (90 ml) Teriyaki sauce, purchased
1 tablespoon (15 g) freshly minced ginger

CHICKEN

1 1/2 pounds (700 g) chicken breasts,
  cubed into 2-inch (5 cm) pieces
1 red bell pepper, cubed
1 green bell pepper cubed
1 red onion, peeled and cubed
6 shiitake mushrooms, stems removed
6 bamboo skewers (9-inch or 20 cm)

STEAMED RICE

2 cups (465 g) Japanese-style rice
2 1/4 cups (535 ml) water

SAUCE

1 tablespoon (15 g) granulated sugar
2 cloves garlic, peeled and chopped
1 shallot, peeled and diced
1 tablespoon (15 g) freshly grated ginger
3 tablespoons (45 ml) sake
1/2 cup (120 ml) Teriyaki sauce, purchased

GARNISH

3-ounces (85 g) Wakame seaweed salad
1 tablespoon (15 g) sesame seeds
  Parsley sprigs

EQUIPMENT

1 small glass or stainless steel bowl
1 small saucepan
Chef's knife and cutting board
Fine mesh strainer
Grill pan or outdoor grill
Rice cooker (or medium saucepan and lid)

Prepare marinade by mixing both ingredients in a small glass or stainless steel bowl.

Slide alternating pieces of chicken and vegetables through skewers and smother with marinade.

Cover and refrigerate for 1 hour.

To make Japanese rice:

Using a rice cooker: Wash rice with cold water, several times, until the water becomes almost clear. Drain rice in a colander and set aside for 30 minutes.

Place rice in rice cooker, add rice and let soak for 1 hour. Start cooker and follow manufacturer's directions.

On the stove top: Wash rice with cold water, several times, until the water becomes almost clear.

Drain rice in a colander and set aside for 30 minutes.

Place rice in a medium saucepan, add water and let soak for 1 hour. Cover and bring to a boil. Reduce heat to low and simmer for 20 minutes or until water is almost gone. Remove from heat and let sit for 5 minutes.

Meanwhile, in a small saucepan over medium heat, caramelize sugar and add garlic, shallot and ginger, deglaze with sake and whisk in teriyaki sauce. Quickly bring to a boil. Remove from heat and pass through a fine sieve. Keep sauce warm.

To grill kebabs:

Outdoor grill: Heat to medium high and place kebabs on grill. Cook each kebab for 5 to 7 minutes, turning only once. Remove from grill and transfer on a platter.

Indoor grill: Heat to medium high and place kebabs on grill. Cook each kebab for 5 to 7 minutes, turning only once. Remove from grill and transfer on a platter.

Cover with aluminum paper and keep warm.

Place a spoonful of Wakame salad on slightly warmed plates. Top with kebab and drizzle with sauce. Finish with sesame seeds.

Serve Japanese rice in individual bowls as a side dish and garnish with parsley.

Serves 6.

Difficulty 3.

Singapore Noodles

CHICKEN AND SHRIMP

3 tablespoons (45 ml) soy sauce
1/4 cup (60 ml) dry white wine
Freshly ground white pepper
2 skinless chicken breasts, thinly sliced
1/2 pound (230 g) shrimp (size 60/90) peeled and deveined

VEGETABLES

3 tablespoons (45 ml) vegetable or canola oil
1 tablespoon (15 g) peeled and grated ginger
1 clove garlic finely chopped
1 medium yellow onion, julienned
2 stalks celery, cut diagonally (Asian cut)
1 red bell pepper, julienned
1 green bell pepper, julienned
2 carrots, julienned
1 small bok choy, 1 1/2" or 3 cm cut diagonally and blanched
2 green onions, cut diagonally
3-ounces (85 g) bean sprouts
Salt and freshly ground white pepper

EGG

1 teaspoon (5 ml) canola oil
2 eggs, beaten

NOODLES

1 pound (450 g) Yakisoba Stir-fry Noodles, dipped in hot water and drained

SAUCE

1 tablespoon (15 ml) canola oil
2 teaspoons (10 g) peeled and grated ginger
2 cloves garlic, finely chopped
1 shallot, finely chopped
2 tablespoons (30 g) Madras curry powder
1 tablespoon (15 g) turmeric
1/2 cup (120 ml) ketchup
1/4 cup (60 ml) pineapple juice
1/3 cup (90 ml) chicken stock
2 tablespoons (30 ml) soy sauce

GARNISH

2 green onions, finely chopped diagonally
1 small white onion, thinly sliced into rings, dusted with flour and deep-fried
Fresh parsley

EQUIPMENT

Chef's knife and cutting board
Medium glass or stainless steel bowl
Slotted spoon
Wok or large sauté pan
Wooden spoon

Prepare marinade in a glass or non-reactive bowl by combining all ingredients. Coat chicken and shrimp with marinade, cover and refrigerate for 20 minutes.

For stir-fry, in a wok over medium-high heat, warm 1 tablespoon (15 ml) oil and sauté ginger, garlic and onions for 3 minutes or until onions are translucent. Add chicken and shrimp and stir-fry for 2 minutes. Remove shrimp and chicken and set aside.

Using the same wok, warm remaining oil and stir-fry celery, peppers and carrots for 3 minutes. Add bok choy, green onions and bean sprouts and stir-fry for 2 minutes. Season with salt and pepper and set aside.

Wipe wok clean and coat with oil. Warm oil over medium-high heat and add beaten eggs. Rotate wok to create a thin pancake-like shape. Cook through and set aside. Roll tight and thinly slice just before serving.

Warm Yakisoba noodles by running them under hot water. Drain thoroughly.

To make sauce, in a wok over medium heat, warm oil and sauté ginger, garlic and shallot for 3 minutes. Do not brown. Add remaining ingredients and bring to a boil. Add chicken, shrimp, noodles and stir-fried vegetables and toss for 2 to 3 minutes to get all ingredients hot.

Divide into warmed plates. Garnish with julienned egg pancake and green onions. Top with fried onions and finish with parsley sprigs.

Serves 4.

Difficulty 3.

Wine Pairing ⌒ Chateau Ste. Michelle, Dry Rosé, "Nellie's Garden", Columbia Valley, Washington

WINE PAIRING ✐ MERLOT, CHARLES KRUG, NAPA, CALIFORNIA

Grilled London Broil

ONION CONFIT

2 medium onions, peeled and shaved
1/3 cup (90 ml) extra virgin olive oil

1 teaspoon (5 g) fresh thyme
2 basil leaves, julienned
1 tablespoon (15 g) chopped parsley

STEAK

2 tablespoons (30 ml) Worcestershire sauce
1/4 cup (60 ml) extra virgin olive oil
1 clove garlic, peeled and shaved
3 pounds (1.4 kg) London broil or flank steak
Salt and freshly ground black pepper

RED ONION JAM

1 tablespoon (15 ml) extra virgin olive oil
3 red onions, peeled and sliced
1 tablespoon (15 g) light brown sugar
1 tablespoon (15 ml) red wine vinegar
2 tablespoons (30 ml) dry red wine
1/4 cup (60 ml) chicken stock (page 172)
Salt and freshly ground black pepper
1 teaspoon (5 g) thyme

MASCARPONE MASHED POTATOES

1 pound (450 g) Yukon Gold potatoes, peeled, quartered
1/4 cup (60 ml) heavy cream
1 tablespoon (15 g) unsalted butter
4-ounces (120 g) mascarpone cheese
Salt and freshly ground white pepper

SHIRAZ GLAZE

1 tablespoon (15 ml) extra virgin olive oil
3 shallots, peeled and chopped
1/4 cup (60 ml) Shiraz wine
1/2 cup (120 ml) veal demi-glace (page 173)

VEGETABLES

2 yellow zucchini, quartered lengthwise
2 portabella mushrooms, thickly sliced
2 tablespoons (30 ml) extra virgin olive oil
Salt and freshly ground black pepper

GARNISH

Thyme sprigs

EQUIPMENT

1 glass baking dish or baking sheet
1 large stockpot or Dutch oven
1 pastry brush
1 potato ricer
1 sauté pan
2 rubber spatulas
2 small glass or stainless steel bowls
2 small saucepans
Chef's knife and cutting board
Chinois or fine mesh strainer
Metal tongs
Outdoor grill or grill pan

In a small saucepan over medium heat, simmer onions in olive oil for 20 minutes. Do not brown. Allow to cool and mix in the fresh herbs. Cover and reserve.

For the meat, mix Worcestershire sauce, olive oil and garlic in a small glass bowl. Season London broil with salt and pepper; place in a shallow pan and coat with oil mixture. Cover and refrigerate.

To make the onion jam, in a sauté pan over medium heat, warm oil and sauté onions for 6 to 8 minutes or until onions have softened. Add sugar and cook for 2 minutes. Deglaze with vinegar and red wine, add chicken stock and simmer for 10 to 12 minutes or until onions have reached a jam consistency and liquid has evaporated. Keep warm.

For mashed potatoes, place potatoes into salted cold water, bring to a boil and cook until potatoes are easily pierced with the tip of a knife, about 15 minutes. Drain and press potatoes through a potato ricer into a heated bowl. Stir in cream, butter and mascarpone cheese.

Adjust seasoning with salt and pepper. Set aside and keep warm.

For Shiraz glaze, in a small saucepan over medium heat, warm oil and sauté shallots for 5 minutes. Deglaze with red wine. Add demi-glace and simmer for 6 to 8 minutes or until reduced by half. Strain and keep warm.

For London broil:

Outdoor grill: Preheat grill for high heat. Place meat on the grill and reduce heat to medium. Cover grill and cook for 5 to 8 minutes on each side depending on the doneness required. Transfer to a serving platter, cover with aluminum foil and let stand for 5 minutes. Cut slices at an angle.

Indoor grill : Preheat oven to 325°F (162°C). Place grill pan in oven and heat thoroughly. Place meat on grill pan and cook for 10 to 15 minutes, depending on desired doneness, turn meat one time during cooking. Transfer to a serving platter, cover with aluminum foil and let stand for 5 minutes. Cut slices on an angle.

To grill the vegetables:

Outdoor grill: Heat to medium high. Brush cut sides of vegetables with olive oil, season with salt and pepper and

place on grill. Cook each slice for 3 to 5 minutes, turning only once. Remove from grill, transfer on a platter, lightly brush with onion confit and fresh herbs, cover and keep warm.

Indoor grill: Lightly oil a grill pan. Set temperature to medium-high heat. Brush cut sides of vegetables with olive oil, season with salt and pepper and place on grill. Cook each slice for 5 minutes, turning only once. Remove from grill, transfer on a platter, lightly brush with onion confit and fresh herbs, cover and keep warm.

To serve, place a heap of mashed potatoes in the center of warmed entrée plate, arrange sliced London broil atop and garnish with portabella mushrooms, a spoonful of onion jam and thyme sprig. Drizzle with Shiraz glaze and finish each dish with a couple slices of grilled yellow zucchini.

Serves 6.

Difficulty 4.

Strawberry Parlova

STRAWBERRY SYRUP

1 cup (230 g) strawberries, quartered
1 cup (230 g) granulated sugar
1 teaspoon (5 ml) vanilla extract
3 tablespoons (45 ml) water

MERINGUES

4 egg whites, room temperature
1 cup (235 g) granulated sugar
1/2 teaspoon (2.5 g) cornstarch
1 teaspoon (5 ml) lemon juice

GARNISH

Whipped cream
6 strawberries, halved
Mint sprigs
6 chocolate cigarettes, purchased
1-ounce (30 g) pistachio, chopped
18 wild strawberries

EQUIPMENT

1 medium glass or stainless steel bowl
1 small saucepan
Baking sheet
Chef's knife and cutting board
Chinois or fine mesh strainer
Hand mixer or wire whisk
Ice cream scoop
Rubber spatula

Preheat oven to 300°F or 150°C.

In a small saucepan over medium heat, combine all ingredients for the strawberry syrup and bring to a boil. Lower heat and simmer for 15 minutes or until berries are soft and syrup is thickened.

Remove from heat and strain through a fine strainer into a clean container. Let cool, cover and refrigerate.

Meanwhile, to make meringues, place egg whites in a stainless steel or glass bowl and, using a hand-held mixer, beat on medium speed until soft peaks form. Gradually

add sugar a little at a time until stiff peaks form. Fold in cornstarch and lemon juice.

Using an ice cream scoop, create balls and delicately transfer on a pre-greased baking sheet. Gently tap the top of each meringue to create a flat surface.

Bake for 30 minutes. Remove from heat and let cool on a wire rack.

To serve, place each meringue on a chilled dessert plate. Top with a dollop of whipped cream, a couple half strawberries, a mint sprig and a chocolate cigarette.

Finish with a drizzle of strawberry syrup. Sprinkle with pistachio and garnish with wild strawberries.

Serves 6.

Difficulty 3.

Toasted Almond Kahlia

1 1/2 oz. (4.5 cl) Kahlúa
1 oz. (3 cl) Amaretto Disaronno Originale
1 1/2 oz. (4.5 cl) half & half

Fill shaker with ice and add all ingredients. Shake well and strain into an ice filled rock glass.

WINE PAIRING ❦ PERRIER-JOUËT, BRUT, CHAMPAGNE, "FLEUR DE CHAMPAGNE BELLE EPOQUE", FRANCE

A CONTEMPORARY BISTRO WITH A DÉCOR OF MOSAIC FROM THE COLIBRI COLLECTION DESIGNED BY SICIS, ONE OF THE MOST FAMOUS MOSAIC COMPANIES IN MILAN, ITALY. OVERSIZED WOOD GARDEN CHAIRS COVERED WITH PLUSH PILLOWS, THE SOOTHING SOUNDS OF WATER FOUNTAINS, SOFT MUSIC AND SUBTLE LIGHTING. DINING AT THE SOLARIUM FEELS LIKE YOU'RE ENJOYING A PICNIC BESIDE A WINDING BROOK.

WITH A PANORAMIC VIEW OF THE SOLARIUM POOL AND OUTDOOR SPACE, ITS CENTRALIZED BUFFET COUNTER, USED AS A

COMBINATION OF BUFFET DURING THE DAY AND AN INTERACTIVE BAR AND DESSERT DISPLAY IN THE EVENING, IS ONE OF THE HIGHLIGHTS OF THE PLACE. THE RESTAURANT GIVES AN INDOOR-OUTDOOR FEEL, WHERE AMBIENT AIR MIXES WITH SUNLIGHT AND COOL BREEZES.

USING THE FRESHEST INGREDIENTS IN FLAVORFUL COMBINATIONS, SOLARIUM OFFERS A WIDE ARRAY OF LIGHT MENU FARE AND UNUSUAL LIBATIONS IN A RELAXING SPA-STYLE SETTING.

Solarium

Vitality

Royal Caribbean International℠

LEAVE A LITTLE ROOM FOR DESSERT! TEMPT YOURSELF WITH OUR LOW-FAT MINI BITES.

START YOUR EXPERIENCE WITH A REFRESHING CUCUMBER MARTINI. ENJOY MOUTH-WATERING CREATIONS FROM AROUND THE WORLD, SUCH AS A PERUVIAN CEVICHE, A MEDITERRANEAN EGGPLANT OR BOUILLABAISSE.

FRESH, LIGHT AND "LITE," IN KEEPING WITH ROYAL CARIBBEAN INTERNATIONAL'S VITALITY℠ PROGRAM, THE DELECTABLE CULINARY SELECTIONS WE HAVE CREATED FOR SOLARIUM ARE DESIGNED WITH MINIMUM CALORIES AND MAXIMUM TASTE IN MIND.

Poached Egg and Frisée Salad

VINAIGRETTE

1/4 cup (60 ml) red wine vinegar
2 tablespoons (30 g) Dijon mustard
Salt and freshly ground black pepper
1/2 cup (120 ml) extra virgin olive oil

EGGS

1 cup (250 ml) water
1 teaspoon (5 ml) lemon juice
6 large eggs

SALAD

1 frisée lettuce, center removed and placed in
chilled water
1 Lollo Rosso lettuce, thickly julienned
1 red Batavia lettuce, center removed
and placed in chilled water
4-ounces (120 g) baby arugula,
placed in chilled water
4-ounces (120 g) mesclun mix
4-ounces (120 g) cherry tomatoes, quartered
2 large yellow heirloom tomatoes, sliced

GARNISH

3-ounces (85 g) croutons, purchased
Cumin powder
Chive whiskers

EQUIPMENT

Chef's knife and cutting board
Coffee saucer
Paper towels
Slotted spoon
Small glass or stainless steel bowl
Small saucepan
Wire whisk

For vinaigrette, in a small stainless steel or glass bowl, combine vinegar, mustard, salt and pepper and mix well. Slowly incorporate oil while whisking constantly to emulsify the ingredients. Cover and refrigerate.

To poach eggs, in a small saucepan over medium heat, bring water and lemon juice to a boil and reduce heat to low. Break each egg into a saucer and gently slip into the simmering water. Cook for 3 minutes. Remove cooked eggs with a slotted spoon and drain over a paper towel.

Arrange assorted lettuce, tomatoes and croutons in chilled plates. Top with a poached egg and drizzle with vinaigrette.

Sprinkle each egg with cumin powder and garnish with chives.

Serves 6.

Difficulty 1.

Chilled Cucumber and Yogurt Soup

CUCUMBER SOUP

2 cups (265 g) cucumbers,
  peeled, seeded and diced
3 cups (710 ml) low-fat Greek yogurt
1/4 cup (60 ml) low-fat sour cream
1 teaspoon (5 g) Dijon mustard
Juice of 1 lemon
Kosher salt and freshly
  ground white pepper

GARNISH

1 cucumber, washed and shaved
Dill sprigs

EQUIPMENT

Chef's knife and cutting board
Food processor or blender
Large glass or stainless steel bowl
Soup ladle

For soup, place all ingredients into a food processor and blend until smooth. Season with salt and pepper.

Transfer into a glass or stainless steel bowl, cover and refrigerate for 2 to 3 hours.

Ladle chilled soup in bowls and garnish with shaved cucumbers and dill sprigs.

Serves 6.

Difficulty 1.

Cucumber Cocktail

2 thin cucumber slices, skin on
1 oz. (3 cl) fresh lime juice
2 oz. (6 cl) gin
1 oz. (3 cl) simple syrup (page 173)

Combine cucumber and lime juice in a mixing glass. Using a muddler, mash cucumber until broken into small pieces. Add gin and simple syrup and transfer into an ice filled cocktail shaker. Shake well, pour into rock glass and garnish with a cucumber wheel.

Peruvian Ceviche

MARINADE

1 medium yellow onion, small diced
4 cloves garlic, finely chopped
2 fresh red chilis, seeded and thinly sliced
1 cup (240 ml) freshly squeezed lime juice
1 cup (240 ml) freshly squeezed orange juice
3 tablespoons (45 ml) extra virgin olive oil
2 teaspoons (30 g) kosher salt
2 tablespoons (30 ml) rice wine vinegar
1/4 bunch cilantro, finely chopped

FISH

12 sea scallops, diced
10-ounces (285 g) basa fish fillet, diced
4-ounces (120 g) cherry tomatoes, quartered
1 small red onion, diced

ROASTED POTATOES

2 sweet potatoes, peeled and sliced lengthwise
2 tablespoons (30 ml) extra virgin olive oil
Salt

GARNISH

1 Belgian endive, base sliced off
and leaves separated
1 radicchio lettuce
2 limes, sliced
Chopped cilantro
Cilantro sprigs

EQUIPMENT

Baking sheet
Chef's knife and cutting board
Large glass or stainless steel bowl
Parchment paper
Pastry brush

Place all ingredients for the marinade into a large glass bowl and mix well. Fold in the scallops and basa fish and mix well. Cover and refrigerate overnight, stirring occasionally.

Preheat oven to 400°F or 205°C.

For potatoes, brush with olive oil and season with salt. Place on a sheet pan lined with greased parchment paper and roast for 15 minutes or until potato slices are tender to the touch and lightly caramelized.

Spoon ceviche into chilled bowls garnished with leaves of Belgian endives, radicchio and roasted sweet potato slices.

Sprinkle with chopped cilantro and decorate with lime slices and cilantro sprigs.

Finish ceviche by folding in the quartered cherry tomatoes and red onion to the marinated fish.

Serves 6.

Difficulty 1.

Basa Fish Fillet in Corn Husk

MARINADE

1/2 cup (120 ml) Worcestershire sauce
1/2 cup (120 ml) lime juice
2 teaspoons (10 g) kosher salt

FISH

2 (6-ounce) (170 g) basa fish fillets cut in half
3 tablespoons (35 g) chipotle powder
1 leek, white part only, julienned and blanched
2 large carrots, peeled, julienned and blanched
2 celery stalks, julienned and blanched
1 red bell pepper, julienned
Salt and freshly ground white pepper
18 corn husks, cleaned and soaked
in boiling water for 1 hour

TOMATO-MANGO COMPOTE

1 tablespoon (15 ml) extra virgin olive oil
1 red onion, chopped
2 cloves garlic, shaved
8-ounces (230 g) cherry tomatoes, halved
1 mango, peeled and chopped
1 chili, deseeded and thinly sliced
1/2 teaspoon (2.5 g) chipotle powder

GARNISH

3 limes
Parsley sprigs

EQUIPMENT

Baking sheet
Chef's knife and cutting board
Large pot or stockpot
Medium stainless steel or glass bowl
Parchment paper
Slotted spoon
Small sauté pan
Spatula

Preheat oven to 400°F or 205°C.

For marinade, mix all ingredients in a stainless steel or glass bowl. Pour over fish fillets, cover and refrigerate for 2 hours.

Remove fish from marinade, sprinkle with chipotle powder, top with julienned vegetables, season with salt and pepper and wrap in corn husks.

Transfer onto a sheet pan lined with greased parchment paper and bake for 10 minutes.

To make compote, in a small sauté pan over medium heat, warm oil and sauté onions and garlic for 3 minutes, add tomatoes, mango and chili and season with chipotle powder. Simmer for 10 minutes or until mixture is thick and both tomatoes and mangoes are soft. Remove from heat and keep warm.

Arrange fish in warmed plates and open husks slightly. Garnish with lime slices and parsley sprigs and serve with a side dish of tomato-mango compote.

Serves 6.

Difficulty 2.

Mediterranean Eggplant

RATATOUILLE

1 tablespoon (15 ml) extra virgin olive oil
2 yellow onions, diced
3 cloves garlic, minced
1 red chili pepper, deseeded and minced
1 16-ounce (450 g) can
    Italian strip tomatoes

3 tablespoons (45 ml) extra virgin olive oil
1 green bell pepper, small cubed
1 red bell pepper, small cubed
1 yellow bell pepper, small cubed
2 zucchini, small cubed
2 yellow squash, small cubed
1/4 bunch fresh basil, julienned
1 tablespoon (15 g) dry oregano
Salt and freshly ground black pepper

EGGPLANTS

3 Japanese eggplants, sliced lengthwise
2 tablespoons (30 ml) extra virgin olive oil
Salt and freshly ground black pepper

GARNISH

1/2 cup shredded mozzarella
3 red chili peppers, halved, seeded and lightly
    grilled
Fresh basil sprigs

EQUIPMENT

Baking sheet
Chef's knife and cutting board
Large sauté pan
Medium sauté pan
Parchment paper
Pastry brush
Serving spoon
Wooden spoon

Preheat oven to 400°F or 205°C.

For ratatouille, in a sauté pan over medium heat, warm olive oil and sauté onions and garlic for 3 minutes. Add tomatoes, chili pepper and salt and cook for 10 minutes or until most of the liquid has been absorbed.

In a large sauté pan over high heat, warm olive oil and sauté vegetables in batches for 5 minutes or until nicely colored. Season with salt and pepper and keep warm.

Place all vegetables back into the sauté pan and bind with tomato sauce. Stir in herbs and finish cooking for 10 minutes or until all vegetables are tender.

Meanwhile, brush eggplants with olive oil and season with salt and pepper. Place onto a sheet pan lined with greased parchment paper and bake for 15 minutes.

Remove from heat and, using a spoon, delicately remove the center of each eggplant.

Fill eggplants with ratatouille, sprinkle with mozzarella and return to the oven for 10 minutes.

Arrange each eggplant on a plate and garnish with a half grilled chili pepper and basil sprig.

Serves 6.

Difficulty 2.

WINE PAIRING ⌒ BODEGAS JULIÁN CHIVITE, ROSADO, NAVARRA, "GRAN FEUDO", SPAIN

Wine Pairing ∾ Pinot Noir, Domaine Drouhin, Willamette Valley, Oregon

Toasted Barley and Mushroom Risotto

RISOTTO

3 tablespoons (45 ml) extra virgin olive oil
1 medium yellow onion, finely chopped
2 cloves garlic, finely chopped
6-ounces (170 g) cremini mushrooms, sliced
8-ounces (230 g) button mushrooms, sliced
6-ounces (170 g) portabella mushrooms, halved then sliced
2 tablespoons (30 g) chopped fresh thyme
1 bay leaf
Salt and freshly ground black pepper
1 1/2 cups (350 g) toasted barley, soaked in water overnight then drained
1 cup (140 ml) dry white wine
6 cups (1.4 L) warm chicken stock

GARNISH

18 green asparagus, peeled and blanched
Parmesan shavings
3 tablespoons (45 g) finely sliced scallions

EQUIPMENT

Chef's knife and cutting board
Large saucepan
Wooden spoon

In a large saucepan over medium heat, warm olive oil and sauté onion and garlic for 3 minutes.

Add cremini, button and portabella mushrooms, thyme and bay leaf and cook for 5 to 7 minutes or until softened. Season with salt and pepper and stir in barley. Cook for 3 minutes, stirring constantly. Add white wine and stir until liquid is completely absorbed.

Incorporate the chicken stock one ladle at a time, stirring frequently after each addition. Wait until the stock is almost completely absorbed before adding another ladle.

After about 18 to 20 minutes, barley should be tender to the bite but still slightly firm in the center and look creamy. Taste and rectify seasoning.

Reheat asparagus by plunging them in boiling water.

Ladle barley risotto in warmed bowls and garnish with asparagus, Parmesan shavings and sliced scallions.

Serves 6.

Difficulty 1.

Passion Papaya Crush

1 1/2 oz. (3.75 cl) papaya juice
1/2 oz. (1.5 cl) passion fruit juice
1/2 oz. (1.5 cl) pineapple juice
Splash of Sprite

Fill cocktail shaker with ice. Add all ingredients except for Sprite. Spindle mix and pour into a pint glass. Top off with Sprite and garnish with a pineapple wedge.

Solarium

Bouillabaisse

BOUILLABAISSE

3 tablespoons (45 ml) extra virgin olive oil
1 large yellow onion, chopped
3 cloves garlic, chopped
2 carrots, peeled and diced
2 zucchini, diced
2 yellow squash, diced
3 stalks celery, diced
1 fennel, shaved
1/3 cup (90 ml) dry white wine
2 pinches saffron threads, soaked
    in 2 tablespoons (30 ml) dry white wine
1 (16-ounce) or (450 g) can of chopped tomatoes
2 bay leaves
3 fresh thyme sprigs
2 fresh rosemary sprigs
1 1/2 quarts (1.4 L) seafood stock
Sea salt and freshly ground black pepper
1 pound (450 g) basa fish fillets, diced
18 sea scallops
12 large shrimp, raw, peeled, deveined, tail on

CROSTINI

1 French bread baguette, sliced
2 cloves garlic
2 tablespoons (30 ml) extra virgin olive oil

GARNISH

Thyme sprigs

EQUIPMENT

Baking sheet
Chef's knife and cutting board
Pastry brush
Soup ladle
Stockpot or large pot
Wooden spoon

Preheat oven to 400°F or 205°C.

For broth, in a large stockpot over medium heat, warm oil and sauté onion and garlic for 3 minutes. Add vegetables and cook for 8 minutes. Do not brown.

Deglaze with white wine and add saffron mixture, tomatoes and herbs. Cook for 3 minutes, stirring occasionally.

Add seafood stock, season with salt and pepper and bring to a boil.

Reduce heat and simmer for 1/2 hour or until vegetables are soft to the touch and liquid has decreased in volume by 1/4. Taste and rectify seasoning.

Add fish and seafood to the soup and poach for 5 minutes.

Meanwhile rub bread slices with garlic and brush with olive oil. Place on a sheet pan and bake for 2 to 3 minutes or until golden around the edges.

Ladle bouillabaisse into warmed bowls. Garnish with fresh thyme sprig and serve with a garlic crostini.

Serves 6.

Difficulty 1.

WINE PAIRING ⸺ PENFOLDS, CHARDONNAY, "KOONUNGA HILL", AUSTRALIA

WINE PAIRING ↬ ROSA REGALE, CASTELLO BANFI, BRACHETTO D' ACQUI, ITALY

Assorted Mini Bites (pages 62-65)

Raspberry Coconut Bars

RASPBERRY BARS
2 pounds (900 g) coconut flakes
1 cup (235 g) granulated sugar or
3/4 cup (175 g) sugar substitute
2 eggs
1/4 cup (60 ml) milk
1 cup (235 g) fresh raspberries

CHOCOLATE GANACHE
1 cup (235 g) dark chocolate
1 cup (240 ml) heavy cream

GARNISH
20 raspberries
20 chocolate triangles, store bought

EQUIPMENT
1 baking sheet
1 small saucepan
2 medium glass or stainless steel bowls
Chef's knife and cutting board
Parchment paper
Spatula
Stand or hand mixer
Wire rack
Wire whisk

Preheat oven to 400°F or 205°C.

Place coconut flakes and sugar in a medium size glass or stainless steel bowl and mix well. Add eggs and milk and beat well using an electric mixer on medium speed.

Transfer coconut mixture into a small sheet pan lined with greased parchment paper and spread evenly. Cover with raspberries and bake for 20 minutes.

Meanwhile, in a small saucepan over low heat, warm chocolate and cream until chocolate has melted. Stir well and transfer into a stainless steel bowl.

Remove cake from oven and allow to cool to room temperature in pan. Transfer to a wire rack and evenly spread the chocolate ganache over the cake top. Refrigerate.

Cut into 3-inch x 1 1/2-inch (7 cm x 3.5 cm) bars. Garnish with raspberries and chocolate triangles.

Serves 8 to 10.

Difficulty 2.

Soy Panna Cotta

SOY PANNA COTTA
1/2 cup water
1 pack, unflavored gelatin powder
3 cups (710 ml) unsweetened chocolate soy milk
1 pinch salt
1 teaspoon (5 ml) vanilla extract
1 cup (235 g) granulated sugar or
3/4 cup (175 g) sugar substitute
1/3 cup (85 g) cocoa powder, sifted

GARNISH
10 dark chocolate molds, purchased
Whipped cream
Zest of 1 orange
Mint leaves
10 dark chocolate half moons, purchased

EQUIPMENT
1 medium saucepan
1 small glass or stainless steel bowl
Ramekins or glass molds
Wire whisk

In a small glass bowl, mix water and gelatin together. Let sit for 2 minutes.

In a medium size saucepan over medium heat, warm soy milk, salt and vanilla extract. Whisk in sugar and cocoa powder and bring to a boil.

Remove from heat and incorporate gelatin. Cool, stirring constantly for 7 to 10 minutes.

Pour cooled chocolate mixture into chocolate molds or individual glass ramekins and refrigerate for 3 hours.

If using individual glass molds, upon serving, remove panna cotta from molds.

Garnish each panna cotta with a dollop of whipped cream, an orange zest, a fresh mint leaf and a chocolate half moon.

Serves 8 to 10.

Difficulty 1.

Mango Yogurt

MANGO CREAM

1 tablespoon (15 ml) water
1/4 pack, unflavored gelatin powder
1 mango, peeled and diced
1/4 cup (60 ml) water
1/3 cup (85 g) granulated sugar or
3 tablespoons (45 g) sugar substitute
1/4 cup (60 ml) heavy cream, whipped

YOGURT

1 32-ounce tub (900 g) organic vanilla
yogurt
3 ripe mangoes, peeled and diced

GARNISH

Mint leaves

EQUIPMENT

1 medium glass or stainless steel bowl
1 small glass or stainless steel bowl
1 small saucepan
Blender or immersion blender
Chef's knife and cutting board
Ice cream scoop

In a small glass bowl, mix water and gelatin together. Let sit for 2 minutes.

For mango cream, mix mango, water and sugar in a small saucepan and simmer for 10 minutes. Remove from heat, transfer into a blender and process until smooth.

Place mixture into a stainless steel or glass bowl and whisk in gelatin. Let cool.

Gently fold in whipped cream and freeze for 1 hour.

To serve, alternate layers of vanilla yogurt and diced mango in individual glasses. Top each dessert with a small scoop of mango cream and garnish with a mint leaf.

Serves 10.

Difficulty 1.

Mini Apple and Ginger Cupcakes

CUPCAKES

2 cups (465 g) all-purpose flour
1 teaspoon (5 g) baking soda
1/4 cup (60 g) granulated sugar or
2 tablespoons (30 g) sugar substitute
1/2 teaspoon (2.5 g) ground cinnamon
1 teaspoon (5 g) ground ginger
1/4 teaspoon (1 g) ground nutmeg
1/4 teaspoon (1 g) salt
2 large eggs
1 cup (235 g) organic apple cider
1/2 cup (115 g) buttermilk
2 small apples, peeled, cored and grated
1 small apple, peeled, cored and thinly
sliced

GARNISH

2 tablespoons sugar-free apricot jam
2 tablespoons water

EQUIPMENT

1 small glass or stainless steel bowl
2 large glass or stainless steel bowls
Large plastic zip lock bag
Mini muffin tins with liners, or
1 baking sheet and mini muffin liners
Pastry brush
Stirring spoon

Preheat oven to 375°F or 190°C.

To make cupcakes, in a stainless steel or glass bowl, mix together flour, baking soda, sugar, cinnamon, ginger, nutmeg and salt.

In a large glass bowl, whisk the eggs, apple cider, buttermilk and grated apples. Incorporate flour mixture and stir until dry ingredients are just moistened. Do not overmix.

Line mini muffin cups with paper liners.

Spoon half of the batter into a zip lock bag. Snip a 1/4-inch corner from the bag and fill paper liners 3/4 full.

Top cupcakes with apple slices and bake for 12 to 15 minutes or until a toothpick inserted in the center comes out clean.

Remove cupcakes from the baking pan, place on a wire rack and allow to cool.

To finish cupcakes, in a small glass bowl, mix apricot jam and water and brush mixture over apple slices.

Serves 10.

Difficulty 1.

Florentine

FLORENTINE

1/2 cup (120 ml) heavy cream
1/2 cup (125 g) granulated sugar or
1/4 cup (60 g) sugar substitute
2 tablespoons (30 g) butter
2 tablespoons (30 ml) honey
1/3 cup (85 g) almonds, sliced
1/3 cup (85 g) candied orange and lemon
1/4 cup (60 g) pitted dates, quartered
1/4 cup (60 g) dried apricots, julienned
1/4 cup candied cherries, quartered

GARNISH

1/2 cup (115 g) semisweet chocolate chips
2 tablespoons (30 ml) heavy cream

EQUIPMENT

1 large glass or stainless steel bowl
2 small saucepans
Chef's knife and cutting board
Individual molds or glasses
Stirring spoons

Preheat the oven to 375°F or 190°C.

To make the Florentine, place the heavy cream, sugar, butter and honey in a small saucepan over medium heat and bring to a simmer. Cook until the mixture reaches 244°F or 118°C. Do not boil.

Remove from heat and transfer into a large glass or stainless steel bowl. Slowly incorporate the remaining ingredients and mix well. Let cool.

Pour mixture into individual molds set in a shallow pan or baking dish. Pour water into the pan until it is halfway up the sides of the molds and bake for 25 minutes.

Let cool entirely before taking pastries off the mold.

Meanwhile, place chocolate chips and cream in a small saucepan over low heat and cook until melted. Do not over heat.

Dip each pastry into melted chocolate and place upside down (chocolate on top) on a rack to cool.

Serves 10.

Difficulty 2.

CASUAL AND CONTEMPORARY, IZUMI RESTAURANT AND SUSHI BAR IS A STYLISH ASIAN BISTRO DECORATED WITH BAMBOO, LIGHT WOOD AND DELICATE WATER LILIES. IT OFFERS A SEA-VIEW VISTA, RELAXING ATMOSPHERE AND JAPANESE-INFLUENCED MENU ITEMS CREATED WITH THE HELP OF CHEF CONSULTANT TRAVIS KAMIYAMA.

WORKING IN TANDEM WITH CHEF TRAVIS, ONE OF LOS ANGELES' MOST RECOGNIZED SUSHI CHEFS, OWNER OF SEVERAL SUCCESSFUL RESTAURANTS AND RENOWNED SUSHI INSTRUCTOR IN CALIFORNIA, WE CREATED A TANTALIZING JAPANESE-STYLE CUISINE INCLUDING EXPERTLY CRAFTED SUSHI, SIZZLING HOT ROCK® AND SIMMERING SUKIYAKI.

SIT AT THE SUSHI BAR TO WATCH OUR SUSHI CHEF OR "TAMAE" PREPARE HIS DELECTABLE CREATIONS; SIP A REFRESHING SAKE MARTINI SERVED BY A WAIT STAFF CLAD IN TRADITIONAL JAPANESE-INSPIRED BLACK-DRESS KIMONOS FROM THE TAISHO PERIOD (1912-1925), RELAX AND ENJOY THE BEST SUSHI ON THE SEVEN SEAS.

Salmon Salad with White Sesame Dressing

SESAME DRESSING

1/4 cup (60 g) white sesame seeds, toasted
1/4 cup (60 g) granulated sugar
3 teaspoons (45 ml) dark soy sauce
1/2 cup bonito stock (page 78)
2 tablespoons (30 ml) ponzu sauce (page 75)
1 teaspoon (5 ml) chili sesame oil

SALAD

1 pound (450 g) salmon, skinless and cubed
3-ounces (85 g) masago
4-ounces (120 g) sprouts
6-ounces (170 g) mesclun
2-ounces (60 g) baby watercress
2-ounces (60 g) frisée lettuce
2 cucumbers, seeded and sliced lengthwise

GARNISH

1 tablespoon (15 g) black sesame seeds
4 teaspoons (20 g) tobiko

EQUIPMENT

2 small glass or stainless steel bowls
Chef's knife and cutting board
Large glass or stainless steel bowl
Small sauté pan

Toast sesame seeds by heating a small sauté pan over low heat and gently tossing seeds until they acquire a golden color. Immediately transfer seeds to small glass or stainless steel bowl and let cool.

For dressing, mix all ingredients in a small stainless steel or glass bowl.

In a large stainless steel or glass bowl, combine all ingredients for the salad and toss with dressing.

Arrange salad in chilled bowls, sprinkle with sesame seeds and garnish with a spoonful of tobiko.

Serves 4.

Difficulty 1.

Tuna Carpaccio

Izumi

GARLIC CHIPS

3 tablespoons (45 ml) extra virgin olive oil
4 cloves garlic, thickly shaved

AIOLI

1 teaspoon (5 g) Dijon mustard
2 cloves garlic, minced
1 egg
1 egg yolk
1 tablespoon (15 ml) freshly squeezed lemon juice
1 cup (240 ml) extra virgin olive oil
Salt and freshly ground white pepper
1 teaspoon (5 g) wasabi powder

TUNA

2 (10-ounce) (285 g) ahi tuna blocks (sashimi grade)
1 tablespoon (15 ml) extra virgin olive oil
Freshly ground black pepper

GARNISH

1 jalapeño pepper, deseeded, halved and thinly sliced
3-ounces (85 g) tobiko
1-ounce (30 g) daikon sprouts

EQUIPMENT

1 small saucepan
Baking sheet
Chef's knife and cutting board
Food processor or blender
Pastry brush
Slotted spoon
Small glass bowl
Spatula

In a small saucepan over low heat, warm oil and cook garlic for 8 minutes or until golden brown. Using a slotted spoon, transfer garlic chips into a plate lined with absorbent paper.

For aioli, in a blender, combine the mustard, garlic, eggs and lemon juice and purée. With the machine running, slowly add the olive oil a little at a time. Season with salt and pepper and add wasabi powder. Transfer into glass bowl, cover and refrigerate.

Using a sharp knife, cut tuna in 1-inch (2.5 cm) thin slices. Brush each slice with olive oil and sprinkle with black pepper.

Arrange tuna slices on chilled plates. Place a dollop of aioli on each tuna slice and garnish with jalapeño and a small mount of tobiko.

Top each tuna slice with a few garlic chips and finish decorating the plates with daikon sprouts.

Serves 6.

Difficulty 2.

Shrimp Wonton Soup

SHRIMP WONTON

2 teaspoons (10 ml) vegetable oil
1 shallot, minced
1 teaspoon grated ginger
8-ounces (230 g) flounder fillets
1 egg white
1 tablespoon (15 g) cornstarch,
dissolved in 1 tablespoon (15 ml) water
1 teaspoon (5 ml) sake
1 teaspoon (5 ml) mirin sauce
Salt
18 medium shrimp, peeled,
deveined, tails off and chopped
18 square wonton wrappers
1 egg, beaten

BROTH

1 quart (1 L) chicken stock (page 172)
1 tablespoon (15 g) shredded ginger
2 scallions, halved
4-ounces (120 g) shiitake mushrooms, quartered
10-ounces (285 g) clear cellophane noodles,
soaked in water for 5 minutes and drained

GARNISH

2 green onions, sliced into thin rings

EQUIPMENT

Chef's knife and cutting board
Food processor
Large pot or stockpot
Medium glass bowl
Medium saucepan
Pastry brush
Slotted spoon
Small glass or stainless steel bowl
Small saucepan

To make wontons, in a small saucepan over medium heat, warm oil and sauté shallot and ginger for 5 minutes.

Place trimmed fish in a food processor and pulse until well-chopped, add egg white, cornstarch, sake, mirin, shallot mixture and salt and mix to a smooth paste. Transfer into a glass bowl and fold in chopped shrimp.

Lightly brush wrappers with beaten egg. Place a spoonful of fish mousse in each wrapper and fold over diagonally, enclosing the mousse to form a triangle. Press the edges of the wrapper to seal. Fold in the 2 corners furthest apart, brush with some beaten egg and press together to seal.

Steam wontons for 5 minutes.

Meanwhile warm chicken stock, ginger, scallions and shiitake mushrooms over medium heat in a large stockpot. Bring to a boil and simmer for 5 minutes. Add cellophane noodles and simmer for 2 minutes or until noodles are warmed through.

To serve, place 3 shrimp wontons in individual warmed bowls, pour in the hot broth and noodles and garnish with green onion rings.

Serves 6.

Difficulty 3.

Assorted Sushi Rolls (pages 74-77)

Foundation and Sauce Recipes

SUSHI RICE

2 cups (465 g) short-grain rice also called shari
2 cups (475 ml) water

SUSHI RICE VINEGAR

1/2 cup (120 ml) rice vinegar
1 tablespoon (15 g) sea salt
2 teaspoons (10 ml) mirin sauce
1/4 cup (60 g) granulated sugar
1 1/2-inch (4 cm) sheet kombu

To make sushi rice, rinse and rub the grains in cold water several times until the water turns from cloudy to clear.

Drain well and transfer to a large saucepan or stockpot. Let stand for 5 minutes. Add water and bring to a boil over high heat. Boil for 1 minute. Reduce heat to low and cook for 5 minutes.

Remove from heat and let rice sit for 15 minutes.

Meanwhile, in a saucepan over medium heat, simmer 1/3 cup (90 ml) rice vinegar, sea salt, mirin and sugar. Do not boil. Add kombu, remove from heat and allow to cool. Stir in remaining rice vinegar.

Transfer cooked rice into a wooden Japanese rice tub (Hangiri) or large glass bowl. Pour 3/4 of the rice vinegar mixture over the rice and mix quickly, while the rice is still hot, with a flat wooden spoon, using a slicing motion. Allow to cool.

Difficulty 2.

HAND VINEGAR

1 cup (240 ml) cold water
2 tablespoons (30 ml) rice vinegar

Mix all ingredients in a medium size glass or stainless steel bowl. Reserve in a glass jar and refrigerate.

JAPANESE MAYONNAISE

2 egg yolks
1/2 teaspoon (2.5 g) salt
Freshly ground white pepper
1 teaspoon (5 g) Dijon mustard
2 teaspoons (30 ml) rice vinegar
1 cup (240 ml) vegetable oil
1 teaspoon (5 ml) chili oil
1 teaspoon (5 g) wasabi powder

Make mayonnaise by beating the egg yolks with a whisk in a small stainless steel or glass bowl, adding the salt, pepper, mustard and rice vinegar, then gradually incorporating the vegetable oil a little at a time. Stir in chili oil and wasabi powder. Cover and chill.

WASABI

3 tablespoons (45 g) powdered wasabi
1 tablespoon (15 ml) water

Add water to wasabi powder in a small glass or stainless steel bowl a little at a time until it reaches a thick paste consistency.

CHAMPAGNE SAUCE

2 egg yolks
1/2 teaspoon (2.5 g) salt
Freshly ground white pepper
1 teaspoon (5 g) Dijon mustard
2 teaspoons (30 ml) rice vinegar
1 cup (240 ml) vegetable oil
3 tablespoons (45 ml) dry Champagne

Make mayonnaise by beating the egg yolks with a whisk in a small stainless steel or glass bowl, adding the salt, pepper, mustard and rice vinegar, then gradually incorporating the oil a little at a time. Stir in Champagne, cover and refrigerate.

PONZU SAUCE

1/4 cup (60 ml) soy sauce
1/2 cup (120 ml) rice vinegar
2 tablespoons (30 ml) freshly squeezed lemon juice
3/4-inch (2 cm) square piece of kombu, wiped clean
1-ounce bonito flakes

Mix all ingredients in a stainless steel or glass bowl. Cover and refrigerate overnight. Strain and reserve in a glass bottle.

Difficulty for sauces 1.

EQUIPMENT FOR RICE

1 flat wooden spoon
1 glass bowl
1 stockpot
1 saucepan
Wooden Japanese rice tub

EQUIPMENT FOR SAUCES

2 small glass or stainless steel bowls
3 medium glass or stainless steel bowls
Sieve or cheesecloth
Small stirring spoons
Wire whisk
Wooden spoon

Boxed Eel

1 teaspoon (5 g) white sesame seeds, toasted
2-ounces (60 g) snow crab meat or Dungeness crab
2-ounces (60 g) crab meat imitation, hand-shredded
1 tablespoon (15 g) Japanese mayonnaise (page 75)
Freshly ground white pepper
1/2 sheet colored soy paper
3-ounces (85 g) sushi rice (page 75)
4 pieces eel

GARNISH
1/4 cup (60 ml) unagi sushi sauce, purchased
Soy sauce
Pickled ginger, store bought
Wasabi (page 75)

EQUIPMENT
Chef's knife and cutting board
Glass or stainless steel bowl
Makisu bamboo roller
Plastic wrap
Sharp sushi knife
Small sauté pan
Sushi box

Toast sesame seeds by heating a small sauté pan over low heat. Add sesame seeds and toss gently until seeds begin to change color. Immediately transfer seeds to small glass or stainless steel bowl and let cool.

In a small glass bowl, mix the crab meat, imitation crab and Japanese mayonnaise. Season with pepper.

With a sushi box:

Press soy paper inside the sushi box and layer with half of the sushi rice. Hand press gently, keeping your hands moistened with hand vinegar (page 75) so that the rice doesn't stick.

Evenly spread crab mixture and cover with remaining rice. Gently press once more.

Top horizontally with eel slices, until it evenly covers the rice.

Squeeze and press hard.

Press through the sushi box onto the plastic wrap-lined makisu bamboo roller.

Reshape as necessary by pressing the bamboo roller against the sushi sides and cut into 6 even pieces. Drizzle with unagi sushi sauce and sprinkle with toasted sesame seeds.

Without a sushi box:

To make roll, cover bamboo mat with plastic wrap. Lay soy paper over plastic wrap and evenly spread sushi rice, keeping your hands moistened with hand vinegar (page 75) so that the rice doesn't stick.

Flip the rice-spread sheet of soy paper over and garnish with crab mixture.

Begin rolling by carefully folding over the top edge and starting the roll. Continue to roll, keeping the roll as tight as possible. Top evenly with eel slices and cut into 6 even pieces.

Drizzle with unagi sushi sauce and sprinkle with toasted sesame seeds.

Serve with soy sauce, pickled ginger and wasabi.

Makes 6 pieces.
Difficulty 2.

Crispy Shrimp Roll

EQUIPMENT
Cast iron skillet or heavy-bottom frying pan
Chef's knife and cutting board
Glass or stainless steel bowl
Makisu bamboo roller
Paper towels
Plastic cling wrap
Sharp sushi knife
Slotted spoon

SHRIMP TEMPURA
1/4 cup (60 g) tempura batter mix, purchased
2 large size shrimp, peeled, deveined, tail on
1/4 cup (60 g) all-purpose sifted flour
1 cup (140 ml) vegetable oil, for frying

ROLL
1/2 sheet seaweed nori
3-ounces (85 g) sushi rice (page 75)
1 small avocado, peeled and sliced
1/4 cup (60 g) crunchy tenkasu flakes

GARNISH
Soy sauce
Pickled ginger, store bought
Wasabi (page 75)

Prepare tempura mix according to the instructions on the package.

Dredge shrimp in flour and shake off any excess.

Dip each piece into the tempura batter and deep-fry in the hot vegetable oil until golden. Drain and place on paper towels.

To make roll, cover bamboo mat with plastic wrap. Lay nori over plastic wrap and evenly spread sushi rice, keeping your hands moistened with hand vinegar (page 75) so that the rice doesn't stick.

Flip the rice-spread sheet of nori over and garnish with avocado slices, spicy Japanese mayonnaise (page 75) and shrimp tempura; with the tails sticking out.

Begin rolling by carefully folding over the top edge. Continue to roll, keeping the roll as tight as possible. Finish by rolling into crunchy tenkasu and cut into 6 to 8 pieces.

Serve with soy sauce, pickled ginger and wasabi.

Makes 6 to 8 pieces.
Difficulty 1.

Vegetarian Roll

1/2 sheet seaweed nori
3-ounces (85 g) sushi rice (page 75)
1 avocado, peeled and thinly sliced
6 asparagus, peeled and blanched
1 cucumber, peeled and julienned
1 carrot, peeled, julienned and blanched
1-ounce (30 g) daikon sprouts
1 tablespoon (15 g) Japanese mayonnaise (page 75)

GARNISH

Soy sauce
Pickled ginger, store bought
Wasabi (page 75)

EQUIPMENT

Makisu bamboo roller
Plastic cling wrap
Sharp sushi knife and cutting board
Small glass bowl

To make roll, cover bamboo mat with plastic wrap. Lay nori sheet over plastic wrap and evenly spread sushi rice, keeping your hands moistened with hand vinegar (page 75) so that the rice doesn't stick.

Flip the rice-spread sheet of nori over and garnish with avocado, asparagus, cucumber, carrots, daikon sprouts and Japanese mayonnaise.

Begin rolling by carefully folding over the top edge. Continue to roll, keeping the roll as tight as possible.

Cut into 6 to 8 pieces.

Serve with soy sauce, pickled ginger and wasabi.

Makes 6 to 8 pieces.

Difficulty 1.

Shrimp Nigiri

6 large size shrimp, raw, tail on
2 tablespoons (30 ml) rice vinegar
1/2 cup (120 ml) water
Sea salt
1 1/3 cups (335 g) sushi rice (page 75)
1-ounce (30 g) wasabi

GARNISH

Soy sauce
Pickled ginger, store bought
Wasabi (page 75)

EQUIPMENT

Makisu bamboo roller
Medium glass bowl
Plastic cling wrap
Sharp sushi knife and cutting board
Slotted spoon
Wooden or steel skewers

Skewer each shrimp on the underside from head to tail to prevent curling and cook for 3 minutes in lightly salted boiling vinegared water. Using a slotted spoon, transfer into iced water.

When cooled, remove skewers, peel, slit the underside of the shrimp open and remove the dark vein.

Moisten your hands with hand vinegar (page 75). Take about 2 tablespoons (30 g) of sushi rice and cradle it in your right hand at the base of your fingers. Gently crush to form a rectangular block about 2-inches (5 cm) long with rounded edges and sides. Scoop up a small amount of wasabi with the tip of your finger and spread it on the bottom center of each shrimp.

Place the shaped rice on top of the wasabi and press gently.

Serve with soy sauce, pickled ginger and wasabi.

Makes 6 pieces.

Difficulty 1.

Lobster Roll

1 sheet colored soy paper
3-ounces (85 g) sushi rice (page 75)
1-ounce (30 g) daikon sprouts
1 avocado, peeled and thinly sliced
3-ounces (85 g) lobster meat
1-ounce (30 ml) Champagne sauce (page 75)
1-ounce (30 g) tobiko

GARNISH

Soy sauce
Pickled ginger, store bought
Wasabi (page 75)

EQUIPMENT

Makisu bamboo roller
Plastic cling wrap
Sharp sushi knife and cutting board
Small glass bowl

To make roll, cover bamboo mat with plastic wrap. Lay colored soy paper over plastic wrap and evenly spread sushi rice, keeping your hands moistened with hand vinegar (page 75) so that the rice doesn't stick.

Flip the rice-spread sheet of soy paper over and garnish with daikon sprouts, avocado slices, lobster meat, a dash of Champagne sauce (page 75) and tobiko.

Begin rolling by carefully folding over the top edge. Continue to roll, keeping the roll as tight as possible.

Cut into 6 to 8 pieces.

Arrange lobster roll on a plate, drizzle with Champagne sauce and serve with side dishes of soy sauce, pickled ginger and wasabi.

Makes 6 to 8 pieces.

Difficulty 1.

Rainbow Roll

2-ounces (60 g) snow crab meat or Dungeness crab
2-ounces (60 g) crab meat imitation, hand shredded
1 tablespoon (15 g) Japanese mayonnaise (page 75)
Freshly ground white pepper
1/2 sheet seaweed nori
3-ounces (85 g) sushi rice (page 75)
1 avocado, peeled and thinly sliced
1 small cucumber, peeled and julienned
1-ounce (30 g) yellowtail, thinly sliced
1-ounce (30 g) sushi grade tuna, thinly sliced
1-ounce (30 g) snapper or tilapia, thinly sliced
1 large size cooked shrimp, peeled, deveined, tail off, and thinly sliced
1-ounce (30 g) fresh water eel, thinly sliced

GARNISH

Soy sauce
Pickled ginger, store bought
Wasabi (page 75)

EQUIPMENT

Makisu bamboo roller
Plastic cling wrap
Sharp sushi knife and cutting board
Small glass bowl

In a small glass bowl, mix the crab meat, imitation crab and mayonnaise. Season with pepper.

To make roll, cover bamboo mat with plastic wrap. Lay nori over plastic wrap and evenly spread sushi rice, keeping your hands moistened with hand vinegar (page 75) so that the rice doesn't stick.

Flip the rice-spread sheet of nori over and garnish with avocado slices, cucumber, crab mixture and spicy Japanese mayonnaise.

Begin rolling by carefully folding over the top edge. Continue to roll, keeping the roll as tight as possible.

Delicately top roll with fish slices, alternating the colors and cut into 6 to 8 pieces.

Serve with soy sauce, pickled ginger and wasabi.

Makes 6 to 8 pieces.

Difficulty 1.

Seafood Sukiyaki

BONITO STOCK

1 20-inch (50 cm) length kelp,
 thoroughly wiped
2.2 quarts (2 L) cold water
3 cups (60 to 80 g) bonito flakes
1/2 cup (120 ml) light soy sauce
1/4 cup (60 ml) mirin sauce
2 tablespoons (30 ml) sake

INGREDIENTS

8-ounces (230 g) salmon, sliced sashimi style
8-ounces (230 g) dolphin fish or sea bream,
 sliced sashimi style
8 sea scallops
8 large shrimp, peeled,
 deveined, tail on
4-ounces (120 g) enoki mushrooms
4-ounces (120 g) shiitake mushrooms,
 washed and stems removed
1 small Chinese cabbage, leaves blanched
4-ounces (120 g) snow peas, blanched
3 large carrots, peeled,
 cut diagonally and blanched
1 block (10-ounce) (285 g) regular tofu,
 cut into large cubes
8-ounces (230 g) cellophane noodles,
 soaked in water for 5 minutes and drained
1 bunch young celery leaves
1-ounce (30 g) white sesame seeds

Serves 4.

Difficulty 1.

EQUIPMENT

2 large pots or stockpots
Chef's knife and cutting board
Fine mesh strainer or Chinois
Nabe pot
Soup ladle
Wooden spoon

For stock, place kelp and 2 quarts of cold water into a stockpot over medium-low heat, and slowly bring to a simmer. Regulate heat so that the water takes approximately 10 minutes to reach a boil.

Remove kelp, add remaining cold water and bonito flakes and quickly bring to a boil.

Remove from heat and skim the surface. Allow bonito flakes to sink to the bottom, about 1 minute and strain liquid through a fine mesh strainer into a large stockpot.

Incorporate the soy sauce, mirin sauce and sake. Return to heat and keep to a simmer.

Arrange all the ingredients in a Nabe pot. Pour in simmering stock, cover and bring to a boil. Cook for 10 minutes and serve with a side dish of rice garnished with white sesame seeds (recipe page 82).

WINE PAIRING ∽ RÉMY PANNIER, VOUVRAY, FRANCE

Izumi

Vegetable Tempura

TENTSYU DIPPING SAUCE

1 cup (240 ml) bonito sauce, purchased
3 tablespoons (45 ml) dark soy sauce
3 tablespoons (45 ml) mirin sauce
1/3 cup (85 g) shredded daikon radish

VEGETABLES

1/2 cup (115 g) tempura batter mix, purchased
1 cup (140 ml) vegetable oil, for frying
1/2 cup (115 g) all-purpose flour, sifted
18 green asparagus, peeled
2 sweet potatoes, peeled and sliced
2 white onions, peeled and thickly sliced
2 zucchini, thickly sliced
2 large carrots, peeled and diagonally sliced
6 large shiitake mushrooms

EQUIPMENT

2 medium glass or stainless steel bowls
Baking sheet
Cast iron skillet or heavy-bottomed frying pan
Chef's knife and cutting board
Paper towels
Slotted spoon
Wire whisk

To make dipping sauce, mix first 3 ingredients in a small stainless steel or glass bowl.

Prepare tempura mix according to the instructions on the package.

For the tempura vegetables, warm oil in a frying pan over medium-high heat.

Dredge vegetables in flour and shake off any excess. Dip each piece into the tempura batter and deep-fry in the hot vegetable oil until golden. Drain and place on paper towels.

Arrange vegetables on warmed plates. Serve with lukewarm tentsyu dipping sauce garnished with a tablespoon (15g) of shredded daikon.

Serves 6.

Difficulty 1.

Hot Rock®

LEMON-GINGER VINAIGRETTE

2 tablespoons (30 ml) lemon juice
2 tablespoons (30 ml) lime juice
3 tablespoons (45 ml) rice vinegar
1 clove garlic, minced
1 teaspoon grated ginger
1 small stalk lemongrass, split open
1/3 cup (90 ml) sweet chili sauce

SWEET SOY SAUCE

1/4 cup (60 g) granulated sugar
3 tablespoons (45 ml) sake
1 cup (240 ml) light soy sauce

SWEET CHILI SAUCE

Sweet Thai chili sauce, store bought

STEAMED RICE

2 cups Japanese-style rice
2 1/4 cups water

HOT ROCK

6 (7-ounce) (200 g) beef tenderloin filets,
cut into 1/2-inch slices
1 broccoli rapini, cut into florets and blanched
6 baby bok choy, blanched
12 crimini mushrooms, cleaned and stems
removed
2 carrots, peeled, julienned and blanched
5-ounces (140 g) bean sprouts

EQUIPMENT

2 small saucepans
6 ceramic ramekins or small serving bowls
6 hot rocks — store bought
Chef's knife and cutting board
Hot rock
Serving platter

For the ginger vinaigrette, in a small saucepan over medium heat, warm lemon juice, lime juice and rice vinegar. Add garlic, ginger and lemongrass and simmer for 5 minutes. Remove from heat. Discard lemongrass and whisk in sweet chili sauce. Transfer into a glass container and let cool. Cover and refrigerate.

For the sweet soy sauce, in a small saucepan over medium heat, warm sugar until it begins to caramelize, stirring constantly, until it turns golden brown. Deglaze with sake, add soy sauce and simmer for 2 minutes. Remove from heat and transfer into a glass container. Let cool. Cover and refrigerate.

To make Japanese rice:

In a rice cooker: Wash rice with cold water, several times, until the water becomes almost clear. Drain rice in a colander and set aside for 30 minutes.

Place rice in rice cooker, add water and let soak for 1 hour. Start cooker and follow manufacturer directions.

In a pot: Wash rice with cold water, several times, until the water becomes almost clear. Drain rice in a colander and set aside for 30 minutes.

Place rice in a small stockpot, add water and let soak for 1 hour. Cover and bring to a boil. Simmer for 20 minutes or until water is almost gone. Remove from heat and let sit for 5 minutes.

Warm hot rocks as per manufacturer's directions.

Arrange beef and vegetables on individual platters and serve with dipping sauces and a side dish of rice.

Serves 6.

Difficulty 1.

WINE PAIRING ∽ PINOT NOIR, ESTANCIA, "PINNACLES RANCHES", MONTEREY, CALIFORNIA

Ginger Crème Caramel

CARAMEL

3 tablespoons (45 g) granulated sugar
1 teaspoon (5 ml) ginger juice
1 teaspoon (5 ml) water

CRÈME

1 1/2 cups (355 ml) milk
1/2 cup (115 g) sugar
2 tablespoons (30 g) freshly grated ginger
4 eggs

GARNISH

Fresh mint leaves

EQUIPMENT

1 small glass or stainless steel bowl
2 small saucepans
2 wire whisks
6 ceramic ramekins
Baking sheet or shallow baking dish
Fine mesh strainer and
cheesecloth or Chinois
Pitcher of tap water (room temperature)
Soup ladle

Preheat oven to 300°F or 150°C.

To make caramel, place all ingredients in a small saucepan over medium heat and cook for 5 minutes or until it starts turning brown. Remove from heat and pour caramel into ramekin bottoms.

In another saucepan, over medium heat, bring milk, sugar and ginger to a boil. Strain through a fine sieve.

In a stainless steel or glass bowl, beat eggs and whisk in the hot milk a little at a time to temper the eggs.

Ladle egg mixture into ramekins and place in a shallow pan or baking dish. Pour water into the pan until it is halfway up the sides of the molds and bake for 40 minutes.

Allow crèmes to cool and refrigerate for 2 to 3 hours.

Upon serving, remove from molds and garnish with mint leaves.

Serves 6.

Difficulty 2.

Green Tea Mousse

MOUSSE

1 gelatin leaf, purchased
1 cup (240 ml) milk
2 egg yolks
1/2 cup (115 g) granulated sugar
1 teaspoon (5 g) macha green tea powder
3 tablespoons (45 ml) water
1 cup (240 ml) heavy cream

GARNISH

Whipped cream
Unsalted pistachios, chopped
6 chocolate butterflies, store bought

EQUIPMENT

2 medium glass or stainless steel bowls
2 wire whisks
Large glass bowl filled halfway with ice
Small glass or stainless steel bowl
Small saucepan
Spatula
Stand mixer or large glass
or stainless steel bowl

To make mousse, place gelatin leaf in a bowl and cover with enough warm water to soften.

Warm milk in a saucepan over medium heat. Remove milk from heat and fold in softened gelatin.

Meanwhile, in a stainless steel or glass bowl, beat egg yolks and sugar together and gradually whisk in milk a little at a time. Dissolve green tea powder in water and add to egg mixture. Stir well, cooling over a bowl of ice.

In a chilled glass or stainless steel bowl, whip heavy cream into stiff peaks and fold into green tea egg mixture.

Divide mixture into glasses and refrigerate for 2 to 3 hours.

To serve, garnish each green tea mousse with a dollop of whipped cream. Sprinkle with pistachios and finish with a chocolate butterfly.

Serves 6.

Difficulty 1.

Asian Fruit Salad with Coconut Sago Dressing

SAGO DRESSING

1/2 cup sago

1 can (13 oz) coconut milk

1 tablespoon (15 g) palm sugar

FRUIT SALAD

1 cup watermelon balls

1 cup honeydew melon balls

1 mango, peeled and thickly sliced

12 fresh lychees, peeled and seed removed

or

1 (1 pound) or (20-ounce) can lychees in syrup

1 yellow star fruit, sliced

EQUIPMENT

2 small saucepans

Chef's knife and cutting board

Fine mesh strainer or Chinois

Medium glass or stainless steel bowl

Parisian scoop or "melon baller"

Wooden spoon

Bring a small saucepan filled with water to a boil and stir in sago. Reduce heat and simmer for 15 minutes or until sago is just transparent. Drain through a sieve and rinse under cold water.

Meanwhile, in a small saucepan over medium heat, mix coconut milk and palm sugar and simmer for 10 to 15 minutes or until syrupy.

Transfer sago to a glass or stainless steel bowl and stir in coconut syrup. Refrigerate.

Arrange fruit in small ramekins and garnish with a spoonful of coconut sago dressing.

Serves 6.

Difficulty 1.

Elderflower Royale

1 1/2 oz (4.5 cl) St. Germain Elderflower liqueur

1/2 oz (1.5 cl) fresh lemon juice

Splash of Champagne

Pour St. Germain Elderflower liqueur and lemon juice in a chilled Champagne glass and top off with Champagne. Garnish with a lemon twist.

Saketini

2 oz (6 cl) gin

3/4 oz (2.25 cl) Sake rice wine

Fill shaker with ice and add all ingredients. Shake well and strain into a chilled martini glass. Garnish with a pitted green olive.

Izumi

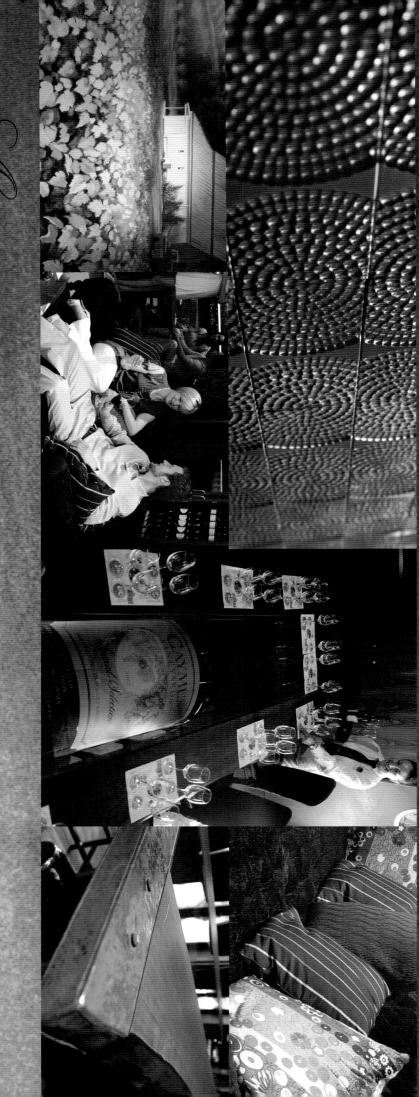

Antique woods and high-back settees, plush velvet, burnished copper and a wine bar for the ages, certainly for carefully aged fine wines.

Don't let the atmosphere distract you from the main attraction in Vintages. Our wonderful wines, tasty tapas and sample wine flights have been created to unite four of the world's most famous names in the history of wine — Robert Mondavi, Caymus, Beringer Blass and Niebaum Coppola.

A feature found nowhere else, Vintages holds the largest handcrafted wine bottle in the world. This one-of-a-kind item was donated by Caymus Vineyards and was designed to be the focal point of the bar.

This bottle holds 152 gallons (575 liters) of wine, has a height of 99.15 inches or 8.26 feet (2.52 meters), a circumference of 79¼ inches (2 meters) at the base and weighs 260 lbs (118 kg) empty and 1,528 pounds (693 kg) full.

Vintages

FIND A COZY CORNER AND GATHER WITH FRIENDS FOR SOME
MOCHA-INFLECTED MERLOT AND ENTICING PLATTERS OF TAPAS.
SAVOR THE TANTALIZING COMBINATIONS OF TASTES AND TEXTURES
AND LET OUR KNOWLEDGEABLE WINE TENDERS LEAD THE WAY.

WINE PAIRING ❧ BODEGAS SIERRA CANTABRIA, RIOJA, CRIANZA, SPAIN

Vintages Tapas (pages 90-95)

Croquetas de Pollo con Revuelto de Cebollinas
(Chicken Croquettes with Chive Rémoulade)

CHIVE RÉMOULADE

1 cup (240 ml) mayonnaise
1 tablespoon (15 ml) Worcestershire sauce
Juice of half lemon
1 teaspoon (5 ml) Tabasco
1 medium yellow onion, diced
2 stalks celery, diced
1 clove garlic, minced
1/4 bunch fresh parsley, chopped
1/2 bunch chive, chopped
Salt and freshly ground black pepper

Preheat oven to 200°F or 95°C.

To make rémoulade, mix all ingredients in a glass or stainless steel bowl. Season with salt and pepper, cover and refrigerate for 4 hours.

In a medium stockpot over medium-high heat, bring chicken stock to a boil. Add chicken quarters and simmer for 20 minutes or until cooked through. Allow to cool, remove skin, pull meat off the bone and dice.

CROQUETAS

2 cups (480 ml) chicken stock
2 chicken quarters, skin on
2 pounds (900 g) Yukon Gold potatoes, peeled and quartered
2 tablespoons (30 ml) olive oil
1 small onion, diced
2 cloves garlic, diced
1 egg yolk
Salt and freshly ground black pepper

Place potatoes into salted cold water, bring to a boil and cook until potatoes are easily pierced with the tip of a knife, about 15 minutes. Drain and transfer into a sheet pan.

Place in the oven for 10 minutes to allow moisture to evaporate.

Meanwhile, in a small sauté pan over medium heat, warm oil and sauté onion and garlic for 4 minutes or until onion is translucent. Do not brown.

CRUST

1/2 cup (115 g) all-purpose flour
1 egg, beaten
1 cup (235 g) breadcrumbs
2 cups (475 ml) canola oil for frying

Press potatoes through a potato ricer into a heated bowl. Add chicken, onion mixture and egg yolk. Season with salt and pepper and mix well. Spread mixture onto a baking sheet and let cool.

Using a spoon, divide mixture into 18 equally sized balls and roll in your hands to make small cylinders. Roll first into flour, then dip in egg and finally into the breadcrumbs. Set aside on a baking sheet lined with parchment paper.

EQUIPMENT

1 glass or stainless steel bowl
4 baking sheets
4 stockpots
Frying pan
Paper towels
Parchment paper
Potato ricer
Small sauté pan
Spoon
Wooden spoon

In a small frying pan over medium-high heat, warm oil and deep fry croquetas in batches, making sure they are completely submerged in hot oil, for 1 to 2 minutes or until golden. Transfer to a paper towel-lined tray and let drain. Season with salt and keep warm in the oven.

Serves 6.

Difficulty 2.

Tortilla de Patatas
(Spanish Potato Omelet)

TORTILLA

5 large Idaho potatoes, peeled, thinly
  sliced and reserved in cold water
3 tablespoons (45 ml) extra virgin
  olive oil
3 white onions, peeled and thinly sliced
6 eggs, beaten
Salt and freshly ground black pepper

GARNISH

Paprika
Parsley sprigs

EQUIPMENT

1 large frying pan
1 sauté pan
1 tray
Chef's knife and cutting board
Paper towels
Non-stick, ovenproof baking dish

Preheat oven to 350°F or 175°C.
For tortilla, blanch potatoes in hot oil.
Drain and place on a paper towel-lined
tray.

In a sauté pan over medium heat, warm
oil and sauté onions for 10 to 15 minutes
or until onions are caramelized. Season
with salt and pepper.

Grease a non-stick, ovenproof baking
dish and layer potatoes and onions
alternatively. Pour in egg batter and
bake for 15 minutes.

Cut tortilla in wedges, sprinkle with
paprika and garnish with parsley.

Serves 6.

Difficulty 1.

Setas a la Parrilla, Pimietos, Calabacín, y Espárragos (Grilled Mushrooms, Peppers, Zucchini and Asparagus Platter)

GARLIC CONFIT

1 head garlic, peeled and shaved
1/3 cup (90 ml) extra virgin olive oil

VEGETABLES

1/3 cup (90 ml) extra virgin olive oil
3 medium portabella mushrooms,
  thickly sliced
15 asparagus, blanched
1 eggplant, thickly sliced
2 zucchinis, cut lengthwise
2 yellow squash, cut lengthwise
Salt and freshly ground white pepper
1 red bell pepper
1 green bell pepper

GARNISH

Chopped parsley

EQUIPMENT

1 grill pan or outdoor grill
1 small saucepan
Chef's knife and cutting board
Metal tongs and spatula
Pastry brush

To make garlic confit, in a small
saucepan over medium heat, simmer
garlic in olive oil for 20 minutes. Do
not brown. Allow to cool. Cover and
reserve.

To grill the vegetables:

Outdoor grill: Heat to medium-high.
Lightly brush cut sides of vegetables
with olive oil, season with salt and
pepper and place on grill. Grill each set
of vegetables for 3 to 5 minutes, turning
only once. Remove from grill, transfer
on a deep platter, and liberally brush
with garlic confit, cover and refrigerate.

Indoor grill: Lightly oil a grill pan.
Set temperature to medium-high heat.
Brush cut sides of vegetables with
olive oil, season with salt and pepper
and place on grill. Grill each set of
vegetables for 5 to 7 minutes, turning
only once. Remove from grill, transfer
on a deep platter, cover and refrigerate.

Arrange vegetables on small chilled
plates and sprinkle with chopped
parsley.

Serves 6.

Difficulty 1.

Pan amb Tomaquet
(Tomato-rubbed Crostinis)

TOASTS

1 sourdough bread, store bought and thickly sliced
3 tablespoons (45 ml) extra virgin olive oil
2 cloves garlic, peeled
6-ounces (170 g) cherry tomatoes, halved
Salt and freshly ground black pepper

EQUIPMENT

1 baking sheet
1 pastry brush
Chef's knife and cutting board

Preheat oven to 400°F or 204°C.

To make toasts, lightly brush bread slices with olive oil, place on a baking sheet lined with greased parchment paper and bake for 2 to 3 minutes or until bread slices are golden.

Allow bread slices to cool and rub first with garlic then tomatoes.

Sprinkle with remaining olive oil and season with salt and pepper.

Arrange on a side plate and serve with remaining tomatoes drizzled with olive oil.

Serves 6.

Difficulty 1.

Sangria

1 bottle (75 cl) red wine
1/3 cup (90 ml) Cointreau or Grand Marnier
1/3 cup (90 ml) gin
1/3 cup (90 ml) dark rum
1/3 cup (90 ml) lemon or orange-flavored vodka
1 1/2 cups (355 ml) orange juice
1/2 cup (115 g) sugar
1 orange, washed and thinly sliced
2 lemons, washed and thinly sliced
1 apple, washed, cored and cubed
2 peaches, washed, pitted and cubed
1 1.8 fl. oz (1L) bottle carbonated lemon-flavored soda

GARNISH

1 orange, sliced
2 limes, sliced

EQUIPMENT

Chef's knife and cutting board
Large glass or plastic serving pitcher

To make sangria, place all ingredients into a large pitcher with the exception of the carbonated lemon-flavored soda. Mix well and refrigerate overnight.

Stir in carbonated lemon-flavored soda just before serving.

Pour sangria into chilled glasses garnished with an orange and lime slice.

Serves 6.

Difficulty 1.

WINE PAIRING ∼ PACO ET LOLA, ALBARIÑO, RIAS BAIXAS, SPAIN

Boquerones en Aceite de Oliva y Zumo de Limón (White Anchovies in Lemon Oil)

1 6-ounce can (170 g) marinated white anchovies, purchased
18 green olives stuffed with red peppers
Fresh parsley

Wrap olives with anchovies and arrange on a small plate. Cover and refrigerate.

Decorate with a parsley sprig at the last minute.

Serve tapas with an assortment of olives and a platter of thinly sliced Serrano ham.

Serves 6.

Difficulty 0.

Pimientos Piquillo Rellones De Queso Feta, y Alcachofas a la Plancha, (Cheese-Stuffed Piquillo Peppers and Grilled Vegetables)

PIQUILLO PEPPERS
1/2 cup (115 g) cream cheese
1/3 cup (85 g) feta cheese, crumbled
2 tablespoons freshly minced parsley or chives
Salt and freshly ground black pepper
1 7.5-ounce can (225 g) whole piquillo peppers, drained

GRILLED VEGETABLES
3 pieces baby artichokes, cleaned and halved
1 medium size eggplant, cut into thin slices
1/4 cup (60 ml) extra virgin olive oil
Salt and freshly ground black pepper

GARNISH
Caper berries
Fresh basil

EQUIPMENT
1 small sauté pan
Baking pan
Chef's knife and cutting board
Grill pan or outdoor grill
Pastry brush

For piquillo peppers, in a small sauté pan over low heat, soften cream cheese. Remove from heat and incorporate feta cheese and fresh herbs. Season with salt and pepper and let cool.

Stuff piquillo peppers with cheese mixture and refrigerate.

Meanwhile, brush artichokes and eggplant slices with olive oil and season with salt and pepper.

Grease a grill pan and heat to medium high. Place vegetables in the pan, marking each side with grill marks.

Place eggplants into a small sheet pan, season with salt and pepper and drizzle with remaining olive oil. Cover and refrigerate.

Remove artichokes from grill and transfer into a small plate. Let cool.

Arrange cheese stuffed piquillo peppers and grilled vegetables on small dishes and garnish with caper berries and fresh basil.

Serves 6.

Difficulty 1.

Cippoline al Vinagre Balsamico (Balsamic Marinated Baby Onions)

1/4 cup (60 ml) extra virgin olive oil
1 tablespoon (15 g) unsalted butter
1 1/2 pounds (700 g) baby onion, peeled
2 tablespoons (30 g) granulated sugar
1 cup (240 ml) balsamic vinegar
1 rosemary sprig
1 cup (240 ml) water

GARNISH
Thyme sprigs

EQUIPMENT
Chef's knife and cutting board
Medium glass bowl
Medium sauté pan

In a sauté pan over medium heat, warm oil and butter. Add onions and sauté for 8 to 10 minutes or until onions are lightly brown on all sides.

Add sugar, vinegar, rosemary sprig and water and bring to a boil. Reduce heat and simmer, uncovered, for about 10 minutes or until onions are al dente.

Transfer onions to a glass bowl. Let cool, cover and refrigerate for 2 hours.

Serve in a small platter and garnish with thyme sprigs.

Serves 6.

Difficulty 2.

Ensalada de Pulpo (Octopus Salad)

OCTOPUS
1 1/2 pounds (700 g) baby octopus or squid
1 large yellow onion, peeled and studded with 5 cloves
2 bay leaves

SALAD
1 small cauliflower cut in small florets and blanched
1 medium yellow onion, peeled and diced
1 green bell pepper, diced
12 small caper berries
1/2 fennel bulb, trimmed and diced
2 cloves garlic, minced
1/4 cup (60 ml) sherry vinegar
Juice of 1 lemon
1/2 cup (120 ml) extra virgin olive oil
Sea salt and freshly ground black pepper

EQUIPMENT
1 large glass or stainless steel bowl
1 stockpot
Chef's knife and cutting board
Slotted spoon

For octopus, in a stockpot over high heat, bring salted water to a boil. Add the octopus, studded onion and bay leaves. Bring back to a boil and simmer for 15 minutes or until tender.

Using a slotted spoon, remove octopus from broth and let cool on a plate.

In a large glass or stainless steel bowl, mix together the salad ingredients. Add octopus and mix well. Season with salt and pepper. Cover and refrigerate for 2 hours.

Serves 6.

Difficulty 1.

Brocheta de Chorizo con Camarones y Vieiras

(Garlicky Seafood and Chorizo Skewers)

GARLIC CONFIT

1 head garlic, peeled and shaved

1/3 cup (90 ml) extra virgin olive oil

KEBABS

12 small wood skewers, soaked in warm water

12 sea scallops

3 spicy chorizo sausages, cut diagonally in thick slices

12 large sized shrimp, peeled, deveined, tail on

1/4 cup (60 ml) extra virgin olive oil

Salt and freshly ground black pepper

GARNISH

Chopped parsley

1 small red onion, halved and lightly grilled

Parsley sprigs

EQUIPMENT

1 small saucepan

12 stainless steel skewers

Baking dish

Chef's knife and cutting board

Grill pan (if outdoor grill is not available)

Pastry brush

In a small saucepan over medium heat, simmer garlic in olive oil for 20 minutes. Do not brown. Allow to cool. Cover and reserve.

Thread the sea scallops and chorizo sausage through their center on skewers. Repeat with the shrimp. Transfer kebabs into a baking dish, brush with garlic confit, drizzle with olive oil and season with salt and pepper. Cover and refrigerate for 2 hours.

To grill kebabs:

Outdoor grill: Heat to medium-high and place kebabs on grill. Cook each kebab for 3 to 5 minutes, turning only once. Remove from grill and transfer on a platter.

Indoor grill: Heat to medium-high and place kebabs on grill. Cook each kebab for 3 to 5 minutes, turning only once. Remove from grill and transfer on a platter.

Sprinkle kebabs with chopped parsley and garnish platter with a grilled onion and some parsley sprigs.

Serves 6.

Difficulty 1.

WINE PAIRING ∽ SOKOL BLOSSER, "EVOLUTION", OREGON

Gazpacho

GAZPACHO

2 cups (480 ml) tomato juice
1/2 cup (120 ml) water
1/4 cup (60 ml) red wine vinegar
1/4 cup (60 ml) extra virgin olive oil
1 small red onion, chopped
2 cloves garlic, chopped
1/4 cup (60 g) breadcrumbs
1 teaspoon (5 g) ground cumin
1 teaspoon (5 g) celery salt
1 tablespoon (15 ml) Worcestershire sauce
Tabasco sauce, to taste

CROSTINIS

1 French baguette, sliced
2 tablespoons (30 ml) extra virgin olive oil

GARNISH

1 small red onion, diced
Parsley

EQUIPMENT

Baking sheet
Chef's knife and cutting board
Chinois or fine mesh sieve
Large glass or stainless steel bowl
Pastry brush

Preheat oven to 350°F or 175°C.

Mix all ingredients into a large glass bowl. Cover and refrigerate overnight.

For crostinis, brush bread slices with olive oil. Place on a baking sheet and bake in the oven until golden around the edges.

Pass gazpacho through a sieve and pour into individual martini glasses.

Garnish with red onion and parsley. Serve with crostinis and an assortment of olives.

Serves 8.

Difficulty 1.

Paella de Marisco (Traditional Seafood, Meat and Saffron Rice Dish)

CHICKEN

1 tablespoon (15 g) sweet paprika
1 teaspoon (5 g) dried oregano
1/4 cup (60 ml) extra virgin olive oil
1 3-pound (1.35 kg) frying chicken, cut into 10 pieces
Salt and freshly ground black pepper

PAELLA

2 tablespoons (30 ml) extra virgin olive oil
2 cloves garlic, peeled and chopped
1 yellow onion, peeled and chopped
2 shallots, peeled and chopped
1 red bell pepper, cubed
1 green bell pepper, cubed
3 cups (700 g) short grain Spanish rice
1/2 cup (120 ml) dry white wine
1 tablespoon (15 g) tomato paste
1 quart (1 L) water or chicken stock (page 172)
5 saffron threads
2 tomatoes, cubed
1/2 cup (115 g) frozen peas
1/3 cup olives, pitted and quartered

SEAFOOD

12 sea scallops
12 to 18 large shrimp, peeled, deveined and tail on
1/2 pound (250 g) squid mix

GARNISH

Chopped parsley

EQUIPMENT

1 large paella pan or large sauté pan
1 medium glass or stainless steel bowl
Chef's knife and cutting board
Stirring spoon

For chicken, mix spices with 2 tablespoons (30 ml) olive oil in a small glass or stainless steel bowl. Rub chicken with spice mixture and refrigerate for 1 hour.

Heat remaining olive oil in a paella pan over medium-high heat and sauté marinated chicken, skin-side down first, on all sides until evenly browned. Season with salt and pepper. Remove from pan and reserve.

In the same pan, heat oil over medium-high heat. Add garlic, onion and shallots and sauté for 3 minutes or until onion is translucent. Add peppers and sauté for 5 minutes. Fold in rice and sir-fry to coat the grains with juices and oil. Deglaze with wine. Add tomato paste

and mix well. Pour in chicken stock, return chicken to pan and simmer for 10 minutes, gently moving the pan around so the rice cooks evenly and absorbs the liquid. Add saffron and tomatoes and simmer for 5 minutes. Add seafood and peas and simmer for another 8 minutes, shaking the pan often but without stirring. Add olives at the last minute.

Serve paella on warmed plates and finish with chopped parsley.

Serves 6.

Difficulty 3.

WINE PAIRING ✑ CODORNÍU, BRUT, CAVA, "CLÁSICO", RESERVA, SPAIN

Sweet Samplers (pages 102-104)

Crema Catalán
(Cream Catalan)

EQUIPMENT
1 baking sheet
1 large glass or stainless steel bowl
1 rubber spatula
1 serving fork
1 wire whisk
3 small saucepans
6 small ramekins or aperitif glasses
Soup ladle
Wooden spoon

CREAM CATALAN
1/4 cup orange juice
2 egg yolks
1/2 cup (115 g) granulated sugar
1/2 tablespoon (7.5 g) cornstarch
1 cinnamon stick
Zest of 1/2 orange
3/4 cup (180 ml) milk

CARAMEL
1/2 cup (115 g) granulated sugar
1/2 cup (120 ml) water
1 teaspoon (5 ml) lemon juice

GARNISH
1 6-ounce can (170 g) mandarins in syrup, drained

In a small saucepan over medium heat, bring orange juice to a boil and reduce by half.

Meanwhile, in a glass or stainless steel bowl, beat egg yolks and sugar until frothy. Add cornstarch, cinnamon stick, orange zest and milk and mix thoroughly. Pour mixture in a small saucepan; incorporate reduced orange juice and slowly heat, stirring constantly until it thickens.

Remove from heat, discard cinnamon stick and ladle mixture into ramekins. Allow to cool and refrigerate for 2 hours.

For caramel, place sugar and water in a small saucepan over medium heat and cook until caramel turns golden. Add lemon juice and remove from heat. Using a greased fork, take a small amount of caramel, drizzle on a greased baking sheet and gently form into a small airy ball. Create as many balls as necessary.

Garnish each cream Catalan with mandarins and a caramel ball.

Serves 6.

Difficulty 2.

Mus de Chocolate con Ron
(Chocolate Mousse)

EQUIPMENT
1 hand mixer or wire whisk
1 large glass or stainless steel bowl
1 rubber spatula
1 small saucepan
1 stirring spoon
6 ramekins or aperitif glasses

MOUSSE
1 cup (240 ml) heavy cream
10-ounces (235 g) bittersweet chocolate chips
2-ounces espresso or strong coffee
2 tablespoons (30 ml) dark rum
2 tablespoons (30 g) unsalted butter

GARNISH
Whipped cream
Chocolate shavings
Chocolate accents, purchased

Combine 3 tablespoons (45 ml) of heavy cream, chocolate, coffee, rum and butter in a small saucepan and melt over simmering water (bain-marie), stirring constantly. Remove from heat and let cool, stirring occasionally.

In a chilled glass bowl, using a hand mixer, beat remaining cream to soft peaks. Fold 1/4 of the whipped cream into the chocolate mixture to lighten it. Fold in the remaining whipped cream. Spoon into glasses and chill for 2 hours.

Garnish with a dollop of whipped cream. Sprinkle with chocolate shavings and finish with chocolate accents.

Serves 6.

Difficulty 1.

Sweet Samplers

Mus de Pistacho
(Pistachio Mousse)

2 egg yolks
1/2 cup (115 g) granulated sugar
1 cup (240 ml) warm milk
1 teaspoon (5 ml) vanilla extract
1/3 cup (85 g) pistachio nuts, chopped
1 tablespoon (15 ml) Crème de Menthe
3/4 cup (180 ml) heavy cream

GARNISH
Chopped pistachio
6 white chocolate dessert half moons,
  purchased
6 raspberries
Mint leaves

EQUIPMENT
1 hand mixer or wire whisk
1 large glass or stainless steel bowl
1 rubber spatula
1 small saucepan
6 ramekins or aperitif glasses
Chef's knife and cutting board

In a saucepan, beat egg yolks and sugar.
Stir in milk and vanilla extract. Cook
over low heat until mixture thickens,
about 3 to 5 minutes.
Remove from heat; add chopped
pistachios and crème de menthe and let
cool, stirring constantly.

In a chilled glass bowl, using a hand
mixer, beat cream to soft peaks. Fold
1/4 of the whipped cream into the
pistachio mixture to lighten it. Fold in
the remaining whipped cream.
Spoon into glasses and chill for 2 hours.
Sprinkle each mousse with chopped
pistachio and garnish each mousse with
a chocolate moon, a raspberry and mint
leaf.

Serves 6.
Difficulty 1.

Torta de Queso y Fresas
(Strawberry Cheesecake)

STRAWBERRY COMPOTE
1 cup (230 g) strawberries, quartered
1 cup (230 g) granulated sugar
1 teaspoon (5 ml) vanilla extract
3 tablespoons (45 ml) water

CHEESECAKE
8-ounces (226 g) cream cheese
1/2 cup (115 g) granulated sugar
1/2 cup (120 ml) heavy cream

MERINGUE
2 egg whites, room temperature
1/4 cup (60 g) granulated sugar

GARNISH
6 wild strawberries

EQUIPMENT
1 hand mixer or wire whisk
1 rubber spatula
2 large glass or stainless steel bowls
2 small saucepans
6 ramekins or aperitif glasses

In a small saucepan over medium
heat, combine all ingredients for the
strawberry compote and bring to a boil.
Lower heat and simmer for 15 minutes
or until berries are soft and syrup is
thickened.
Remove from heat, let cool, cover and
refrigerate.

For cheesecake, in a small saucepan over
medium heat, soften cream cheese and
incorporate sugar.

In a chilled glass bowl, using a hand
mixer, beat cream to soft peaks. Fold
1/4 of the whipped cream into the
mixture to lighten it. Fold in the
remaining whipped cream.

To make meringue, place egg whites in a
stainless steel or glass bowl and, using a
hand-held mixer, beat on medium speed
until soft peaks form. Gradually add
sugar a little at a time until stiff peaks
form.

Fold into the cheese mixture.

Fill each glass half way, spoon a small
amount of strawberry compote and
finish with another spoonful of cheese
mixture. Refrigerate for 2 hours.

Garnish with a spoon of strawberry
compote and a wild strawberry.

Serves 6.
Difficulty 3.

Vintages

D INING AT 150 CENTRAL PARK OOZES SOPHISTICATION AND STYLE. THE FINE BONE CHINA COMMISSIONED FROM RAYNAUD OF LIMOGES, THE AMAZINGLY DESIGNED ART NOUVEAU-STYLE MENUS, IMPECCABLE SERVICE, ELEGANTLY DECORATED TABLES AND INCREDIBLE FOOD COME TOGETHER WITH THE PROMISE OF AN UNFORGETTABLE EXPERIENCE.

150 CENTRAL PARK HAS AN IMPRESSIVE, CONTEMPORARY MULTI-COURSE MENU THAT CHANGES SEASONALLY. THIS TASTING-STYLE MENU IS CREATED WITH DISTINCTIVE INGREDIENTS AND PRESENTED WITH UNIQUELY SHAPED SPOONS AND SMALL PLATES ON PLATTERS OF BONE CHINA AND GLASS TO CREATE AN EXPERIENCE LIKE NO OTHER.

150 Central Park

A SPECIAL FEATURE EXCLUSIVE TO 150 CENTRAL PARK
IS THE WIDE ARRAY OF IMPORTED SEA SALTS. EACH HAS
A UNIQUE COLOR AND FLAVOR THAT ENHANCES THE
FOOD AND ELEVATES IT TO UNEXPECTED HEIGHTS.

ADD A MOST EXCLUSIVE WINE LIST, ALONG WITH
UNIQUE FRUIT-INFUSED WATERS TO ENHANCE THE
UNIQUELY PERFECT DINING EXPERIENCE, AND VOILA!

Cauliflower Panna Cotta

PANNA COTTA

2 tablespoons (30 g) unsalted butter
8-ounces (230 g) cauliflower, trimmed
and cut into large florets
1 1/2 cups (355 ml) water
1 cup (240 ml) heavy cream
Salt and freshly ground white pepper
1 sheet gelatin

TUILE

1/3 cup (65 ml) egg whites
2 tablespoons (30 g) sugar
1/3 cup (65 g) all-purpose flour
1/3 cup (65 g) butter, melted
1 teaspoon (5 g) salt
1/2 teaspoon (2.5 g) freshly ground black pepper

GARNISH

2-ounces (60 g) beluga caviar, store bought
Chives

EQUIPMENT

2 medium glass or stainless steel bowls
4 molds or ramekins
Chef's knife and cutting board
Food processor or blender
Parchment paper
Pastry cooling rack
Rubber spatula
Standard baking sheet
Stockpot or heavy saucepan
Wire mesh strainer and cheesecloth
Wire whisk

Preheat oven to 400°F or 205°C.

For panna cotta, in a stockpot or heavy saucepan, over medium heat, melt butter and sauté cauliflower for 2 minutes. Add water and simmer for 20 minutes or until most of the liquid has evaporated. Add cream and simmer for 10 minutes or until cream has reduced by half and cauliflower is fully cooked.

Transfer into a food processor and blend until completely smooth. Strain through a cheesecloth and season with salt and pepper.

Soak gelatin in cold water for 2 minutes. Whisk softened gelatin into cauliflower mixture and spoon into molds. Refrigerate for 2 to 3 hours.

To make tuiles, in a stainless steel or glass bowl, mix all ingredients together. Spread mixture into elongated crescent shapes onto a baking sheet lined with greased parchment paper. Bake for 5 to 7 minutes or until golden brown.

Remove tuiles from oven and transfer on a pastry rack to cool.

Garnish each panna cotta with a tuile and top with a spoonful of caviar and chive sprig.

Serves 4.

Difficulty 3.

WINE PAIRING ∽ MOËT & CHANDON, BRUT, CHAMPAGNE, "IMPÉRIAL", FRANCE

Beet Trio

PICKLED BEETS

1/2 cup (120 ml) apple cider vinegar
1 tablespoon (15 ml) water
1 tablespoon (15 g) sugar
2 teaspoons (10 g) salt
3 bunches yellow baby beets,
washed, peeled and julienned

BEET ICE CREAM

3 large red beets, washed and halved
1 cup (240 ml) orange juice
2 1/2 cups (595 ml) heavy cream
1/2 vanilla bean, sliced lengthwise
12 egg yolks
3/4 cup (175 g) sugar

ROASTED BEETS

3 bunches red and pink baby beets,
washed, trimmed and halved
1/3 cup (85 g) extra virgin olive oil
2 tablespoons (30 g) thyme
Kosher salt and freshly ground black pepper

GARNISH

5-ounces (140 g) mesclun greens
3-ounces (85 g) soft goat cheese
2 tablespoons (30 ml) extra virgin olive oil
Salt and freshly ground black pepper
Fresh parsley sprigs

EQUIPMENT

1 glass or stainless steel bowl
2 medium glass or stainless steel bowls
2 standard baking sheets
Airtight container or glass
mixing bowl with cover
Aluminum foil
Chef's knife and cutting board
Food processor or blender
Measuring cups and measuring spoons
Rubber spatula and wire whisk
Small saucepan
Wooden spoon

Preheat oven to 375°F or 190°C.

For pickled beets, mix vinegar, water, sugar and salt together in a glass or stainless steel bowl. Place beets into an air tight container and cover with vinegar mixture. Seal container and refrigerate overnight.

To make ice cream, lay beets on a greased sheet pan and roast in the oven for 1 1/2 to 2 hours or until a knife inserted in the center of a beet slides in and out without resistance.

Remove from oven and let cool.

Peel beets, chop and transfer into a food processor. Add orange juice and purée until smooth.

Meanwhile in a small saucepan over medium heat, warm heavy cream and vanilla. Bring to a scald and remove from heat.

In a stainless steel or glass bowl, whisk egg yolks and sugar together. Stir into cream mixture, return to stove and cook over low heat, stirring continuously for about 10 minutes or until mixture thickens enough to coat the back of a spoon. Remove from heat and stir in beet mixture. Transfer into a glass container and allow to cool. Place into the freezer and gently stir mixture for a few seconds every 5 minutes for the first half hour to avoid the formation of ice crystals. Freeze for 2 to 3 hours.

For roasted vegetables, lay beets on half of a large sheet of aluminum foil, drizzle with olive oil and sprinkle with thyme. Season with salt and pepper. Fold foil tightly to make a pouch and place onto a sheet pan.

Bake for 45 minutes to 1 hour or until a knife inserted in the center of a beet slides in and out without resistance. Remove from oven, let cool and peel.

Serve a sample of each beet on long chilled plates. Garnish each plate with a mound of mesclun, a slice of goat cheese drizzled with olive oil and seasoned with salt and pepper and fresh parsley.

Serves 6.

Difficulty 5.

Tomato Tart Tatin

TOMATOES

1/2 cup (120 ml) extra virgin olive oil
8 large plum tomatoes, peeled, seeded and quartered
2 tablespoons (30 g) granulated sugar
Salt and freshly ground black pepper

ONIONS

1 tablespoon (15 ml) extra virgin olive oil
1 tablespoon (15 g) butter
2 large red onions, thinly sliced
1 tablespoon (15 g) brown sugar
2 tablespoons (30 ml) red wine vinegar
2 tablespoons (30 ml) apple cider vinegar
1 teaspoon (5 g) minced tarragon
Salt and freshly ground black pepper

PESTO

3/4 cup (175 g) tightly packed basil leaves, blanched and dried
1 clove garlic
1 teaspoon (5 g) toasted pine nuts
2 tablespoons (30 g) grated Parmesan cheese
1/2 cup (120 ml) extra virgin olive oil

PASTRY

1 sheet puff pastry, store bought, thawed and cut into 4 4-inch (10 cm) circles
1 egg yolk, beaten with 1 teaspoon (5 ml) water

CHEESE MOUSSE

3/4 cup (175 g) goat cheese
3/4 cup (175 g) ricotta cheese
1 egg white
2 tablespoons (30 ml) heavy cream
1 tablespoon (15 g) honey
3 tablespoons (45 g) pesto
2 tablespoons (30 ml) extra virgin olive oil

GARNISH

2-ounces (60 g) assorted micro greens
4 basil leaves
1 tablespoon (15 ml) aged balsamic vinegar

EQUIPMENT

Chef's knife and cutting board
Food processor or blender
Medium glass bowl
Medium sauté pan
Parchment paper
Salad fork
Small sauté pan
Tart mold with removable bottoms, size 4-inch or 10 cm

Preheat oven to 260°F or 126°C.

In a sauté pan over high heat, warm oil and toss tomatoes for 2 minutes. Season with salt and pepper. Remove from heat and let sit for 5 minutes.

Grease tart molds with butter and sprinkle with sugar and salt. Layer each mold with 8 pieces of tomato. Place onto a baking sheet lined with greased parchment paper and bake for 40 minutes.

In a small sauté pan over medium heat, warm oil and butter and sauté onions for 5 minutes. Add brown sugar and cook for 8 to 10 minutes or until onions are nicely browned. Deglaze with vinegar and cook until liquid has almost evaporated. Fold in tarragon and season with salt and pepper.

For pesto, place all ingredients into a food processor and blend until smooth. Set aside.

Once the tomatoes are cooked, bring oven temperature up to 400°F or 204°C.

Meanwhile place pastry circles on a greased parchment-lined sheet pan and refrigerate for 20 minutes.

Pierce surface of pastry circles several times with a fork and brush with egg mixture. Bake for 15 minutes or until lightly browned.

For cheese mousse, place all ingredients in a food processor and blend until smooth. Transfer into a glass bowl, cover and refrigerate.

To serve, arrange pastry circles in the center of chilled appetizer plates, spread with cheese mousse and top with caramelized onions and a mound of tomatoes. Garnish with micro greens and a basil leaf. Decorate the plates with drizzles of pesto and balsamic vinegar around the tomato tarte tatin.

Serves 4.

Difficulty 4.

WINE PAIRING ⌘ BOTTEGA VINAIA, PINO GRIGIO, TRENTINO, ITALY

WINE PAIRING ❦ TREANA, VIOGNIER/MARSANNE, "MER SOLEIL VINEYARD", CENTRAL COAST, CALIFORNIA

Sunchoke Cream with Parmesan Froth

SOUP

1 tablespoon (15 g) unsalted butter
2 yellow onions, diced
3 stalks celery, diced
1 pound (450 g) sunchokes
(Jerusalem artichokes), peeled and sliced
1 clove garlic, minced
1 shallot, minced
1/4 cup (60 ml) dry white wine
2 cups (475 ml) chicken stock (page 172)
1 cup (240 ml) heavy cream
Salt and freshly ground white pepper

FROTH

1 cup (240 ml) 2% milk
5 peppercorns, cracked
3 thyme sprigs
1 cup (235 g) grated Parmigiano Reggiano
2 teaspoons (10 g) salt

GARNISH

Tarragon leaves and flowers

EQUIPMENT

Chef's knife and cutting board
Food processor or blender
Heavy pot or stockpot
Large glass or stainless steel bowl
Large saucepan
Small saucepan
Small sauté pan
Wire whisk
Wooden spoon

In a heavy bottom stockpot over medium heat, melt butter and sauté onions and celery for 3 minutes or until onion is translucent. Add sunchokes, garlic and shallots and cook for 2 minutes. Deglaze with white wine and add chicken stock. Bring to a boil and simmer for 25 to 30 minutes or until sunchokes are tender to the touch. Transfer into a food processor and blend until smooth.

Pour mixture into a clean pot, whisk in heavy cream and bring to a simmer. Adjust seasoning with salt and pepper. Remove from heat and keep warm.

For froth, in a small saucepan over medium heat, combine 1/4 cup (60 ml) milk, peppercorns and thyme and warm until milk bubbles around the edges. Whisk in cheese and season with salt. Transfer into a glass bowl and let cool.

Just before serving, in a small sauté pan over high heat, mix a small amount of cheese mixture and milk and whisk briskly until warm and frothy. Repeat as many times as necessary.

To serve, pour soup into warmed soup bowls and garnish with a spoonful of froth and tarragon leaves.

Serves 4.

Difficulty 2.

Gnocchi with Chanterelles

GNOCCHI

1 1/2 pounds (700 g) Idaho potatoes, peeled and quartered
1 cup (235 g) all-purpose flour
2 egg yolks
2 tablespoons (30 ml) canola oil
1/2 teaspoon (2.5 g) salt
2 tablespoons (30 g) melted butter

Or

3 pounds (1.4 kg) potato gnocchi, store bought

CANDIED BACON

8-ounces (230 g) bacon
1/4 cup (60 g) brown sugar

THYME BUTTER

1/2 cup (115 g) unsalted butter
1 tablespoon (15 ml) extra virgin olive oil
8-ounces (230 g) chanterelle mushrooms
1/8 cup (30 ml) dry white wine
2 teaspoons (10 g) fresh thyme
Salt and freshly ground white pepper
Juice of half lemon

MARSALA FOAM

2 teaspoons (10 g) gelatin
1/2 cup (120 ml) 2% milk
1/4 cup (60 ml) Marsala wine
Salt

GARNISH

Chopped fresh parsley
Fresh sage leaves

EQUIPMENT

2 small glass or stainless steel bowls
Chef's knife and cutting board
Immersion blender or hand mixer
Large glass or stainless steel bowl
Large pot or stockpot
Parchment paper
Potato ricer
Silpat or standard baking sheet
Slotted spoon
Small saucepan
Wire whisk

Preheat oven to 375°F or 126°C.

Place potatoes into salted, cold water, bring to a boil and cook until potatoes are easily pierced with the tip of a knife, about 15 minutes.

Spread 1/4 cup (60 g) flour on a clean, dry surface. Using a ricer, press potatoes, while still hot, over flour. Let cool. Form a well in center.

In a bowl, beat egg yolks, salt and canola oil and pour mixture into potato well. Work potato and egg mixture together to combine, working from inside the well outward until the mixture is completely incorporated. Gently knead mixture together with both hands until it begins to form a ball. Add flour as necessary to make the dough thick enough to roll.

Roll the dough into finger-thick cylinders and cut crosswise into 1 1/2 inch pieces.

Press each piece into the curve of a flour-dusted fork and roll gently to shape the gnocchi.

Place potatoes into salted, cold water, bring to a boil and cook until potatoes are easily pierced with the tip of a knife, about 15 minutes.

Place bacon slices on a silpat or a parchment paper-lined sheet pan, sprinkle with sugar and bake for 15 minutes or until crisp. Drain and place on a sheet pan lined with paper towels. Once cool, dice and keep in a dry area.

For sauce, in a small saucepan over medium heat, melt 1 tablespoon (15 g) butter and olive oil and sauté mushrooms for 5 minutes. Deglaze with wine. Add thyme, and season with salt and pepper. Remove from heat and keep warm.

Cook gnocchi in a large pot of lightly salted boiling water. When gnocchi rise to the surface, remove pot from heat, add 1 glass of cold water to stop the cooking process, and remove gnocchi with a slotted spoon or skimmer. Gently toss gnocchi with melted butter into a large stainless steel bowl.

Finish thyme sauce by whisking remaining butter a little at a time. Incorporate lemon juice at the last minute.

For Marsala foam, mix gelatin with milk in a small glass bowl and let sit for 10 minutes. Transfer into a small saucepan and warm over low heat, until lukewarm. Remove from heat and stir in Marsala and salt. Mix with a hand blender until frothy.

To serve, toss gnocchi with thyme sauce and candied bacon and arrange on warmed plates. Finish with chopped parsley, a drizzle of Marsala froth and fresh sage.

Serves 4.

Difficulty 4.

WINE PAIRING ⌒ LOUIS JADOT, CHARDONNAY, MEURSAULT, FRANCE

WINE PAIRING ⌒ S. A. PRÜM, RIESLING, SPÄTLESE, "GRAACHER HIMMELREICH", MOSEL, GERMANY

Seared Scallops with Citrus Purée and Veal Reduction

CITRUS POTATO PURÉE

3 cups (710 ml) heavy cream
2 Russet potatoes, peeled and diced
2 tablespoons (30 g) butter
1 teaspoon (5 g) lemon zest
1 teaspoon (5 ml) lemon juice
1/2 teaspoon (2.5 g) lime zest
1/2 teaspoon (2.5 g) orange zest
Salt and freshly ground white pepper

BACON

5-ounces (140 g) bacon,
fat trimmed and finely chopped

SPINACH

1 teaspoon (5 ml) vegetable oil
1 teaspoon (5 g) butter
1 shallot, minced
1 clove garlic, minced
8-ounces (230 g) baby spinach
Salt and freshly ground white pepper

SAUCE

1/2 cup (120 ml) veal demi-glace (page 173)
2 tablespoons (30 g) butter

SCALLOPS

1 tablespoon (15 ml) vegetable oil
6 sea scallops

GARNISH

2 oranges, peeled and segmented
Parsley sprigs

EQUIPMENT

Chef's knife and cutting board
Medium sauté pan
Potato ricer
Rubber spatula
Small saucepan
Small sauté pan
Small stockpot or heavy saucepot
Wire whisk
Wooden spoon

To make citrus potatoes, in a small stockpot over medium heat, combine heavy cream and potatoes and bring to a simmer. Cook for 10 minutes or until potatoes are soft to the touch. Strain, reserving the liquid in a glass bowl.

Press potatoes through a potato ricer into a heated bowl. Stir in butter, citrus zests and juice and reserved cream a little at a time, stirring constantly, until the mashed potatoes have reached the consistency of a semi soft purée. Season with salt and pepper and keep warm.

For bacon, in a sauté pan over medium heat, cook bacon until crispy. Drain and transfer on a paper towel-lined plate.

In a sauté pan over medium heat warm oil and butter and sauté shallots and garlic for 4 minutes. Do not brown. Add spinach and cook for 3 minutes or until wilted. Season with salt and pepper.

Meanwhile, in a small saucepan over medium heat, bring veal demi-glace to a simmer. Remove from heat and whisk in butter a little at a time.

For scallops, in a sauté pan over medium-high heat, warm oil and sauté scallops for 4 minutes turning once.

Spoon a small amount of citrus purée on warmed plates in a swiping motion, center scallop atop and arrange a spoonful of bacon on one side of the scallop and a bundle of wilted spinach on the other side.

Garnish scallop with a couple orange segments and parsley sprigs and delicately place a little of the veal reduction into the purée cavity.

Serves 6.

Difficulty 3.

Flirtini

1 oz. (3 cl) peach schnapps
1 oz. (3 cl) cranberry juice
1 oz. (3 cl) pineapple juice
1 oz. (3 cl) Champagne

Fill shaker with ice and top with first 3 ingredients. Shake and strain into a chilled Champagne glass. Top with Champagne and garnish with a cherry.

Horseradish Crusted Salmon
and Sweet Mustard Sauce

DILLED CUCUMBER

1 bunch dill, finely chopped
2 teaspoons (30 ml) freshly squeezed
lemon juice
1/2 teaspoon (2.5 g) salt
1/2 teaspoon (2.5 g) granulated sugar
1 teaspoon (5 ml) extra virgin olive oil
1 English cucumber, peeled and julienned

MUSTARD SAUCE

1/4 cup (60 g) Dijon mustard
1 tablespoon (15 g) honey
2 tablespoons (30 ml) Champagne

PARSNIP PURÉE

2 parsnips, peeled and diced
2 quarts (1.8 L) water or vegetable stock (page
172)
1/4 cup (60 ml) heavy cream
2 tablespoons (30 g) butter
1 teaspoon (5 g) freshly grated horseradish
Salt and freshly ground white pepper

SALMON

1/4 cup panko breadcrumbs
2 tablespoons (30 g) freshly grated horseradish
Salt and freshly ground white pepper
6 (4-ounce) (120 g) salmon medallions
2 tablespoons (30 g) Dijon mustard
2 tablespoons (30 ml) vegetable oil

GARNISH

2 tablespoons (30 ml) vegetable oil
Dill sprigs

EQUIPMENT

9" x 13" (23 x 33 cm) glass
or ovenproof baking dish
Chef's knife and cutting board
Food processor or stand mixer
with wire whisk attachment
Large pot or stockpot
Medium glass or stainless steel bowl
Small glass or stainless steel bowl
Small saucepan
Wooden spoon

Preheat oven to 375°F or 190°C.

For cucumber, place first 5 ingredients into a glass or
stainless steel bowl and mix well. Add cucumber, cover
and refrigerate for 2 hours.

To make sauce, mix all ingredients together in a small
glass or stainless steel bowl. Cover and refrigerate.

For purée, place parsnips into salted cold water or
vegetable stock, bring to a boil and cook until parsnips
are easily pierced with the tip of a knife, about
15 minutes. Strain, transfer into a food processor
and blend until smooth. Add in cream, butter and
horseradish. Season with salt and pepper and pulse
a few times to incorporate. Set aside and keep warm.

For salmon crust, place breadcrumbs, horseradish and
seasoning in a food processor and blend until smooth. Pat

dry salmon and brush each medallion with Dijon mustard.
Gently dip into breadcrumb mixture and lightly shake
to remove excess.

Place medallions on a greased baking pan and bake for
6 to 7 minutes or until desired doneness is achieved.

Warm a small amount of oil in a small saucepan. Gently
drop dill sprigs in oil and fry for about 5 seconds. Remove
and place on paper towel to drain.

Place a spoonful of parsnip purée in the center of warmed
plates and crown with a salmon medallion. Arrange a small
amount of dilled cucumber next to the purée, drizzle with
mustard sauce and garnish salmon with fried dill.

Serves 6.

Difficulty 3.

WINE PAIRING — LA CREMA, CHARDONNAY, RUSSIAN RIVER, CALIFORNIA

WINE PAIRING ✑ CRAGGY RANGE, MERITAGE, "TE KAHU GIMBLETT GRAVELS VINEYARD", HAWKES BAY, NEW ZEALAND

Wagyu Strip Steak, Shiitake Bacon, Celery Root Cream and Demi-Glace

SHIITAKE "BACON"

5-ounces (140 g) shiitake mushrooms, thinly sliced
1/3 cup (90 ml) canola oil
Salt

CELERY ROOT CREAM

1 pound (450 g) Idaho potatoes, peeled and cubed
1/2 pound (250 g) celery root, peeled and cubed
2 tablespoons (30 g) butter, cubed
1 cup (240 ml) heavy cream
Salt and freshly ground white pepper

WAGYU STEAK

3 (1 pound) (450 g) Wagyu or Kobe strip steaks
Salt and freshly ground black pepper
1 tablespoon (15 ml) vegetable oil

RED WINE DEMI-GLACE

1/4 cup (60 g) butter
1 small yellow onion, finely chopped
1/4 cup (60 ml) red wine
1/2 cup (120 ml) veal demi-glace (page 173)

GARNISH

Chervil sprigs

EQUIPMENT

2 baking sheets
Aluminum foil
Chef's knife and cutting board
Food mill or potato ricer
Large glass or stainless steel bowl
Large saucepan
Large stockpot
Silpat or parchment paper
Small saucepan
Wire whisk
Wooden spoon

Preheat oven to 325°F or 163°C.

For the shiitake bacon, place mushrooms in a large glass or stainless steel bowl. Add oil and salt and mix well. Transfer on a baking sheet lined with silpat and spread evenly. Bake for 30 minutes or until crisp.

Meanwhile, place potatoes in a stockpot with enough cold salted water to cover them by 2 inches. Bring to a boil and cook for 5 minutes. Add celery root and simmer for 15 minutes or until vegetables are very tender to the touch. Drain well and push through a food mill fitted with the medium size disk into a saucepan. Stir in butter and heavy cream. Season with salt and pepper and keep warm.

For steaks, preheat broiler for 5 minutes over high heat. Broil seasoned steaks to the desired degree of doneness,

about 10 minutes for rare and 14 minutes for medium. Transfer to a warmed platter, tent loosely with aluminum foil and let stand for 10 minutes.

For sauce, in a small saucepan over medium heat, melt 1/2 tablespoon (7.5 g) butter and sauté onion for 3 minutes. Deglaze with red wine and reduce by half. Stir in veal demi-glace and simmer for 10 minutes. Remove from heat and whisk in butter a little at a time.

Cut steaks diagonally in thick slices and place atop celery root cream. Top with shiitake bacon and finish with a spoonful of red wine demi-glace and fresh chervil.

Serves 6.

Difficulty 3.

Park 150 Martini

3 thin cucumber slices, skin on
2 large basil leaves
3/4 oz. (2.25 cl) lemongrass syrup
2 oz. (6 cl) sweet & sour mix
1 1/2 oz. (4.5 cl) vodka

Place the top 3 ingredients in a mixing glass and muddle. Pour into a cocktail shaker filled with ice. Add sweet & sour mix and vodka and shake. Strain into a chilled martini glass and top off with a basil leaf.

Banana Ice Cream with White Chocolate
Banana Crêpe and Tipsy Cherries

ICE CREAM

6 large bananas, peeled
1 1/4 cups (300 ml) heavy cream
1 cup (240 ml) milk
1/2 cup (115 g) granulated sugar
1 vanilla bean, split
5 egg yolks

CHERRIES

1/2 cup (120 ml) port wine
1 tablespoon (15 g) sugar
4-ounces (120 g) fresh cherries, pitted and halved

CRÊPE BATTER

1/2 cup (115 g) all-purpose flour, sifted
Pinch of salt
1 egg
1/4 cup (60 ml) water
1/2 cup (120 ml) milk
2 tablespoons (30 g) unsalted butter

ROASTED BANANAS

2 tablespoons (30 g) unsalted butter
1/3 cup (85 g) granulated sugar
3 bananas, peeled and diagonally cut in 4

CRÊPE FILLING

1/2 cup (115 g) white chocolate chips, chopped
2 tablespoons (30 g) butter

GARNISH

6 chocolate shaped drops, purchased

EQUIPMENT

2 medium glass or stainless steel bowls
2 small heavy saucepans
Chef's knife and cutting board
Crêpe pan
Food processor or immersion blender
Ice cream machine
Large glass or stainless steel bowl
Large mixing bowl
Medium heavy saucepan
Medium sauté pan
Rubber spatula
Slotted spoon
Small glass or stainless steel bowl
Wire whisk
Wooden spoon

To make banana ice cream, place bananas, cream, milk, half of the sugar and vanilla bean in a large saucepan. Cover and heat slowly for 12 minutes. Remove bananas from liquid, transfer to a food processor and purée for 2 to 3 minutes or until smooth. Reserve 1/4 of this purée for crêpe filling. Bring cream mixture back to a simmer.

In a medium glass or stainless steel bowl, beat egg yolks and remaining sugar for 5 minutes or until creamy. Add 3/4 of the banana purée and slowly incorporate milk mixture, whisking continually. Transfer into a saucepan and simmer over medium heat for 8 minutes or until mixture thickens.

Fill a large glass bowl with ice cubes. Place a small glass bowl on top of the ice and strain mixture into the bowl to chill. Once completely cooled, pour mixture into an ice cream machine and process as directed by manufacturer.

In a small saucepan over medium heat, mix port wine and sugar and stir well. Bring to a simmer and add cherries. Poach cherries for 8 to 10 minutes, then transfer to a glass

bowl using a slotted spoon. Bring the remaining port mixture to a boil, reduce heat and simmer until port has reduced by half. Pour over cherries, cover and refrigerate.

For crêpe batter, whisk together the flour, salt and egg in a large mixing bowl. Gradually add water and milk, stirring continuously until mixture is smooth.

For roasted bananas, in a sauté pan over medium heat, melt butter and sugar and sauté bananas for 5 to 7 minutes, turning often or until bananas have caramelized.

To make crêpe filling, heat chocolate chips and butter in a small saucepan over low heat until chocolate is melted. Remove from heat and stir in remaining banana purée. Transfer to a small glass bowl and reserve.

Heat a crêpe pan or non-reactive pan over medium heat. Melt butter and pour into crêpe batter. Mix well. Pour a scoop of batter onto pan and tilt in a circular motion to spread the batter evenly. Cook crêpe for about

1 minute or until the sides of the crêpe turn a light brown and bubbles form in the center of the crêpe. Loosen with a spatula, flip and cook the other side. Stack crêpes on a large plate.

Line crêpes with filling and fold. Position crêpes in the center of dessert plates and top with a scoop of banana ice cream fitted into a chocolate drop. Finish with a couple pieces of caramelized banana and a spoonful of tipsy cherries.

Serves 6.

Difficulty 5.

Wine Pairing ⊂ Graham's Porto. "Six Grapes", Douro, Portugal

Close your eyes, take a sip of our famous Ocean' Rita, relax and imagine yourself beachside at Cape Hatteras or Bar Harbor.

Inspired by colorful, casual seaside cafés, with low-hanging, colorful fishing tackle, surfboards, weathered wood tables, Adirondack chairs and authentic surf music, Seafood Shack serves a variety of the ocean's bounty, and more, in a lively, fun atmosphere.

From traditional gumbos and chowders to an array of steamed, fried or broiled fish and seafood ... if you love seafood, surf's up!

But don't just leave it at that! Try our slow-cooked, tender BBQ ribs, smothered in our own special BBQ sauce and end your feast with a double-chocolate cake.

Take a stroll along the boardwalk! Then, maybe a round on the carousel!

Seafood Shack

Gumbo

ROUX

1/4 cup (60 g) butter
1/4 cup (60 g) all-purpose flour

GUMBO

5-ounces (140 g) chorizo sausage,
 cut into 1/4" slices
2 tablespoons (30 ml) vegetable oil
2 medium yellow onions, peeled and chopped
1 red bell pepper, chopped
1 yellow bell pepper, chopped
1 green bell pepper, chopped
2 stalks celery, chopped
2 cloves garlic, peeled and chopped
1/2 pound (250 g) okra, ends trimmed
 and sliced in 1/2" thick pieces
1/4 cup (60 g) tomato paste
1 tablespoon (15 g) dried basil
1 tablespoon (15 g) dried thyme
2 tablespoons (30 g) gumbo file spices, purchased
2 bay leaves
1 cup (240 ml) dark beer
1 quart (1 L) fish stock (page 172)
Salt and freshly ground black pepper

SEAFOOD

1/2 pound (250 g) crawfish, cleaned
1/4 pound (125 g) crab meat
1/2 pound (250 g) medium size shrimp,
 peeled, deveined and tail off

GARNISH

1/4 bunch parsley, minced
6 sourdough bread bowls, purchased

EQUIPMENT

Chef's knife and cutting board
Large stockpot
Slotted spoon
Small glass bowl
Small saucepan
Wire whisk
Wooden spoon

Make roux by melting butter in a small saucepan over medium heat. Whisk in flour and simmer for about 15 minutes or until nicely browned, stirring constantly. Remove from heat and transfer into a glass container.

For gumbo, in a large stockpot over medium heat, cook chorizo for 5 to 7 minutes or until lightly browned. Using a slotted spoon, remove sausage to a paper towel-lined plate.

Return stockpot to heat, add oil to sausage fat and sauté onions, peppers and celery for 4 minutes or until celery is soft. Add garlic and okra and cook for 5 minutes or until okra turns a dark green color. Stir in tomato paste, herbs and spices.

Incorporate the beer, then the stock, stirring continuously. Add crawfish and sausage, season with salt and pepper and bring to a boil.

Fold in the roux a little at a time whisking gently to incorporate fully. Reduce heat and simmer for 45 minutes. Skim the top of the stew with a clean spoon as needed.

Add crab meat and shrimp to the gumbo and simmer for 5 to 7 minutes or until shrimp are pink.

Remove gumbo from heat, stir in parsley and ladle into carved sourdough bowls.

Serves 6.

Difficulty 3.

Wine Pairing ✒ Michel Redde, Sancerre, "Les Tuilières", France

WINE PAIRING ⸱ MER SOLEIL, CHARDONNAY, SANTA LUCIA HIGHLANDS, CALIFORNIA

Grilled Cajun Seafood Platter

ONION CONFIT

1/2 head of garlic, peeled and shaved
2 medium onions, peeled and shaved
1/3 cup (90 ml) extra virgin olive oil

VEGETABLES

7-ounces (200 g) snow peas
1 cup (235 g) frozen corn kernels

MASHED POTATOES

1 pound (450 g) Yukon Gold potatoes,
      peeled, quartered
1/3 cup (90 ml) heavy cream
1 tablespoon (15 g) unsalted butter
Salt and freshly ground white pepper

LEMON BEURRE BLANC

1 teaspoon (5 ml) extra virgin olive oil
2 shallots, minced
1 small onion, diced
3 tablespoons (45 ml) freshly squeezed
      lemon juice
1/4 cup dry white wine
3/4 cup (175 ml) fish stock (page 172)
1/4 cup (60 ml) heavy cream
3/4 pound (340 g) cubed unsalted butter
Salt and freshly ground black pepper

SEAFOOD

6 3-ounce white fish fillet such as
      butterfish or catfish
3 calamari tubes, laved and
      1 side cut criss-crossed
12 sea scallops
12 shrimp, peeled, deveined and
      tails left on (size 16/20)
1/4 cup (60 g) Cajun spice mix, store bought
1/4 cup (60 g) butter

GARNISH

2 carrots, peeled
3 limes, halved, sprinkled with
      Cajun spices and lightly sautéed in butter

EQUIPMENT

2 small saucepans
Blender or immersion blender
Chef's knife and cutting board
China cap or fine mesh strainer
Japanese mandolin
Large glass or stainless steel bowl
Large sauté pan
Large stockpot
Potato ricer
Wire whisk
Wooden spoon

Preheat oven to 350°F or 175°C.

In a small saucepan over medium heat, simmer garlic and onions in olive oil for 20 minutes. Do not brown. Allow to cool. Cover and reserve.

Blanch snow peas in boiling salted water for 2 minutes and corn kernels for 5 minutes. Remove from water and immediately plunge into ice water. Drain and reserve.

For mashed potatoes, place potatoes into salted cold water, bring to a boil and cook until potatoes are easily pierced with the tip of a knife, about 15 minutes.

Meanwhile, to prepare beurre blanc, in a saucepan over medium heat, warm oil and sauté shallots and onion for 4 minutes. Do not brown. Deglaze with lemon juice and white wine. Add fish stock, bring to a simmer and slowly reduce liquid by half. Add cream and simmer for 10 minutes or until sauce coats the back of a wooden spoon. Do not boil. Blend and strain through a fine sieve and whisk in cold butter a little at a time. Season with salt and pepper. Set aside and keep warm.

Drain and press potatoes through a potato ricer into a heated bowl. Stir in cream and butter. Adjust seasoning with salt and pepper. Set aside and keep warm.

Rub fish and seafood with Cajun spices.

In a large sauté pan over medium heat, melt butter and pan-sear the fish and seafood until golden. Transfer into a greased parchment lined sheet pan and keep warm in the oven with the door slightly ajar.

Reheat vegetables by plunging in boiling water for 2 minutes. Drain well and sauté in small saucepans over medium heat and warmed onion confit for 2 minutes. Season all vegetables with salt and pepper.

Peel the carrots and using a Japanese mandolin slice the carrots lengthwise as thin as possible. If a mandolin is not available slice the carrots lengthwise and then cut the slices into thin threads one slice at a time. Place in a bowl of ice water.

To serve, arrange a small mound of mashed potatoes on each plate and top with fish and seafood. Garnish with snow peas, corn kernels and sautéed lime. Drizzle with lemon beurre blanc and top shrimp with a nest of carrots.

Serves 6.

Difficulty 4.

Fish and Chips

COLESLAW AND DRESSING

1/2 cup (115 g) mayonnaise or
mayonnaise substitute, store bought
2 tablespoons (30 ml) milk
1 tablespoon (15 ml) white wine vinegar
1/2 teaspoon (2.5 g) sugar
1/4 teaspoon (1.2 g) salt
1/8 teaspoon (0.5 g) paprika
1/8 teaspoon (0.5 g) dry mustard
1/8 teaspoon (0.5 g) celery salt
Dash of freshly ground white pepper
1 medium head of cabbage, shredded
1 green bell pepper, shredded
1 large celery stalk, shredded
1 large carrot, peeled and shredded
1 small onion, minced
Or 1 package coleslaw mix, store bought

BATTER

1 cup (235 g) all-purpose flour
3 pounds Idaho potatoes, peeled,
cut into sticks and reserved in cold water
1 teaspoon (5 g) baking powder
1 teaspoon (5 g) salt
1 teaspoon (5 g) freshly ground white pepper
1 egg
3/4 cup (180 ml) milk
1/4 cup (60 ml) beer

CHIPS

2 cups (475 ml) vegetable oil, for frying

FISH

2 cups (475 ml) vegetable oil, for frying
2 pounds (900 g) cod fillet
cut into 3-ounce (85 g) portions
Salt and freshly ground white pepper
1/2 cup (115 g) tempura flour

TARTAR SAUCE

1 cup (235 g) mayonnaise or substitute
1 medium onion, grated
2 dill pickles, minced
1 tablespoon (15 g) chopped fresh dill
1 tablespoon (15 g) chopped fresh parsley

GARNISH

3 lemons, quartered

EQUIPMENT

2 cast iron skillets or large frying pans
2 large glass or stainless steel bowls
2 small glass or stainless steel bowls
Chef's knife and cutting board
Fork or metal tongs
Medium glass or stainless steel bowl
Slotted spoon or fish spatula
Wire whisk

To make coleslaw dressing, place all ingredients in a small
stainless steel or glass bowl and whisk well.

In a large bowl, gently toss prepared vegetables with
dressing. Season to taste, cover and refrigerate.

For the fish batter, in a medium glass or stainless steel
bowl incorporate all dry ingredients and stir until well
mixed. Whisk in egg and slowly add milk and beer
stirring gently, ensuring there are no lumps.

Preheat oil to 350°F or 175°C in a large frying pan over
high heat.

Pat dry fish fillets, season with salt and pepper and
dredge in tempura flour, shaking off any excess.

Dip each piece into batter and gently lay fish in the hot
vegetable oil. Fry until golden brown, turning only once.
Drain and place on a paper-lined plate.

For fries, preheat oil to 350°F or 175°C in a large frying
pan over high heat. Fry fries until golden using a fork
or cooking tongs to separate fries if necessary. Drain and
place on a paper-lined plate. Season with salt and pepper.

Make tartar sauce by mixing all ingredients in a small
stainless steel or glass bowl.

Arrange fish and chips on a paper-lined basket and serve
with a side dish of coleslaw and tartar sauce. Garnish
with lemon wedges.

Serves 6.

Difficulty 2.

Ocean'Rita

1 1/4 oz (3.75 cl) Patrón silver tequila
3/4 oz (2.25 cl) blue Curacao.
2 oz (6 cl) margarita mix

Combine all ingredients in a cocktail shaker filled with ice.
Spindle mix and pour into a salt-rimmed margarita glass.
Garnish with a lime wedge.

Seafood Shack

WINE PAIRING ⟶ CRAGGY RANGE, MERITAGE, "TE KAHU GIMBLETT GRAVELS VINEYARD", HAWKES BAY, NEW ZEALAND

Barbeque Ribs with Baked Beans, Coleslaw and Sweet Potato Fries

BAKED BEANS

16-ounce (450 g) package dry navy beans, washed, stones removed and soaked in cold water overnight
1 quart (950 ml) water
1 teaspoon sea salt
1/3 cup (85 g) dark molasses
1/3 cup (85 g) brown sugar
2 teaspoons (10 g) dry mustard
Salt and freshly ground black pepper
1 medium onion, studded with 3 whole cloves
4-ounces (120 g) piece salt pork, with rind slashed

RIBS

1 quart (950 ml) chicken or beef stock (page 172 & 173)
4 pounds (1.8 kg) baby back ribs
1 cup (240 ml) BBQ sauce, purchased

SWEET POTATO FRIES

2 pounds (900 g) sweet potatoes, peeled and cut into 1/2" or 1.2 cm wide sticks
1/4 cup (60 ml) extra virgin olive oil
1/2 teaspoon (2.5 g) paprika
Salt

COLESLAW AND DRESSING

1/2 cup (115 g) mayonnaise or mayonnaise substitute, store bought
2 tablespoons (30 ml) milk
1 tablespoon (15 ml) white wine vinegar
1/2 teaspoon (2.5 g) sugar
1/4 teaspoon (1.2 g) salt
1/8 teaspoon (0.5 g) paprika
1/8 teaspoon (0.5 g) dry mustard
1/8 teaspoon (0.5 g) celery salt
Dash of freshly ground white pepper
1 medium head of cabbage, shredded
1 green bell pepper, shredded
1 large celery stalk, shredded
1 large carrot, peeled and shredded
1 small onion, minced
Or 1 package coleslaw mix, store bought

EQUIPMENT

Chef's knife and cutting board
2 large glass or stainless steel bowls
Baking sheet
Dutch oven or large pot with lid
Glass or ovenproof baking dish
Large pot or stockpot
Parchment paper
Pastry brush
Slotted spoon
Soup ladle
Spatula

Preheat oven to 250°F or 125°C.

Place beans in a Dutch oven filled with salted water and quickly bring to a boil. Reduce heat to low, cover and simmer for 1 hour.

Stir in molasses, 1/4 cup (60 g) sugar and mustard. Season with salt and pepper and tuck onion and salt pork into beans.

Cover and bake for 5 hours, adding more water as needed to keep beans moist.

Remove the lid. Sprinkle the top of the baked beans with remaining brown sugar and bake for an additional 30 minutes.

For ribs, place stock in a large stockpot over high heat and bring to a boil. Add ribs and simmer for 1 hour or until almost tender.

Remove ribs from stock, cut slab into several 2 ribs pieces and place in a baking dish.

Glaze ribs with BBQ sauce and bake at 325°F or 165°C for 20 to 30 minutes or until fork-tender, brushing often with sauce and turning occasionally.

To make coleslaw dressing, place all ingredients for the dressing in a stainless steel or glass bowl and whisk well.

In a large bowl, gently toss prepared vegetables with dressing. Rectify seasoning, cover and refrigerate.

To make sweet potato fries, place potato sticks on a baking sheet lined with parchment paper. Rub with oil and season with paprika and salt.

Bake for 30 minutes at 425°F or 220°C until lightly browned. Transfer into a paper-lined platter and serve warm.

Ladle baked beans and coleslaw into serving ramekins and serve on a plate with a mound of ribs. Place potato fries in paper cone and serve with your favorite beer.

Serves 6.

Difficulty 4.

Fried Calamari

PESTO CREAM

2 cups (465 g) fresh basil, packed
1/4 cup (60 g) pine nuts
4 cloves garlic, chopped
1/3 cup (85 g) grated Parmesan cheese
1/2 cup (120 ml) olive oil
1/2 cup (120 ml) heavy cream, whipped

BATTER

1 1/2 cups (350 g) all-purpose flour
2 teaspoons (10 g) cornstarch
1/4 teaspoon (1 g) baking powder
1/2 teaspoon (2.5 g) salt
1 1/2 cups (355 ml) beer
1/4 teaspoon (1 g) freshly ground black pepper
1/4 teaspoon (1 g) paprika
2 cloves garlic, minced
1/4 bunch parsley, finely chopped
2 tablespoons (30 g) extra flour

CALAMARI

2 pounds (900 g) squid body meat,
cleaned, sliced into 1/2" rings
1/4 pound (125 g) squid tentacles, cleaned
2 tablespoons (30 g) all-purpose flour

FRENCH FRIES

1 cup (240 ml) canola oil for frying
2 pounds (900 g) Russet potatoes, peeled,
sliced baton like and preserved in cold water
1/2 teaspoon (2.5 g) garlic salt
1/4 teaspoon (1 g) paprika

GARNISH

3 lemons, halved

EQUIPMENT

2 large glass bowls
Cast-iron skillet or heavy-bottom frying pan
Chef's knife and cutting board
Food processor or blender
Metal tongs or fork
Paper towels
Rubber spatula
Wire whisk

Preheat oven to 200°F or 95°C.

Preheat deep fryer to 375°F or 190°C.

For pesto, place basil leaves in small batches in food processor and whip until finely chopped. Add 1/2 of the nuts and garlic and blend again. Add 1/2 of Parmesan and blend slowly adding 1/2 of the oil, stopping to scrape down sides of the blender. Repeat until all ingredients are used. Process mixture until it forms a smooth paste.

In a chilled glass bowl, whip heavy cream until it forms soft peaks. Fold in basil pesto a little at a time until desired color and taste is achieved. Cover and refrigerate.

Transfer remaining pesto, if any, into a plastic container with a lid. Pesto will keep fresh for 2 to 3 weeks in the refrigerator or can be frozen for months.

To make batter, combine flour, cornstarch, baking powder and salt in a glass or stainless steel bowl. Add remaining ingredients and whisk well ensuring there are no lumps.

Pat dry squid and squid tentacles and dust with flour. Working in small batches of 5 to 7 pieces of squid at a time, dip and coat each ring in batter and gently drop into deep fryer. Cook for 4 minutes or until golden brown, using a fork or cooking tongs to separate calamari rings if necessary.

Drain on a paper-lined plate. Keep calamari warm and crisp by placing them into the warmed oven, leaving the door open while frying the remaining batches.

For French fries, warm oil over medium-high heat in a large frying pan. Pat dry fries, season and transfer in hot oil, using a fork or cooking tongs to separate fries if necessary. Fry for 4 to 5 minutes or until golden. Drain on a paper-lined plate and season with salt.

Arrange fries in a cone or basket and top with fried calamari. Serve with halved lemons and pesto cream on the side.

Serves 6.

Difficulty 2.

WINE PAIRING ⌒ ERRÁZURIZ, SAUVIGNON BLANC, LATE HARVEST, CASABLANCA VALLEY, CHILE

Double Chocolate Cake

GANACHE

1 pound (450 g) dark chocolate, broken into pieces
2 cups (500 ml) heavy cream

SIMPLE SYRUP

1/4 cup (60 g) granulated sugar
1/3 cup (60 ml) water

CAKE

2 cups (465 g) all-purpose flour
1 3/4 cups (410 g) granulated sugar
3/4 cup (175 g) cocoa
1 1/4 teaspoons (7 g) baking soda
1/2 teaspoon (2.5 g) double acting baking powder
1 teaspoon (5g) salt

1 1/4 cups (300 ml) milk
3/4 cup (175 g) shortening
3 eggs
1 teaspoon (5 ml) vanilla extract

GARNISH

Whipped cream
8 strawberries, sliced and fanned
1/4 cup (60 g) small chocolate shavings

EQUIPMENT

3 small saucepans
2 9-inch or 23-cm round cake pans
Chef's knife and cutting board
Large glass or stainless steel bowl
Pastry brush
Rubber spatula
Serrated knife
Spatula
Stand mixer or hand mixer
Wire rack
Wire whisk

Preheat oven to 350°F or 175°C.

For ganache, in a small saucepan over low heat, warm chocolate and cream until chocolate has melted. Stir well and transfer into a stainless steel bowl; cover and refrigerate.

Prepare syrup by mixing all ingredients in a small saucepan and boiling until sugar has melted. Let cool.

For cake, place first 6 ingredients in a large stainless steel or glass bowl, and mix well. Add remaining ingredients and, with a hand mixer at low speed, beat until well mixed, constantly scraping the sides of the bowl. Bring mixer to high speed and mix for 3 additional minutes. Spoon mixture into 2 pre-greased round cake pans and bake for 30 to 35 minutes or until the tip of a knife inserted into the cake comes out clean. Remove from oven and let cool in the cake pans for 10 minutes. Remove from pans, place cakes on wire racks and cool completely.

Using a serrated knife, slice off the middle top of each cake, brush each slice with sugar syrup and spread the bottom of each slice with a fine coat (1/2-inch or 1 cm) of cold ganache, placing each slice on top of the others.

In a small saucepan over low heat, warm remaining ganache. Evenly spread over the cake top and sides. Refrigerate.

To serve, cut cake into triangles, arrange on chilled dessert plates and sprinkle with chocolate shavings. Garnish with a dollop of whipped cream and a strawberry fan.

Serves 8.

Difficulty 2.

Torrential Tea

1/2 oz (1.5 cl) vodka
1/2 oz (1.5 cl) Mount Gay Eclipse silver rum
1/2 oz (1.5 cl) gin
1/2 oz (1.5 cl) triple sec
2 oz (6 cl) sweet & sour mix
1/2 oz (1.5 cl) Midori melon liqueur
Splash of Sprite

Place all ingredients except Sprite and Midori liqueur in a shaker. Add ice and shake well. Pour into a pint glass and top off with Midori liqueur and Sprite. Garnish with a lemon wedge.

$\mathscr{R}$oyal Caribbean's signature steakhouse, known for its great steaks and friendly, professional service.

The ambience and décor is inspired by a 1920s Chicago scene with a mural commissioned to an artist whose specialty is to create backdrops for popular movies such as "The Pirates of the Caribbean" and "Charlie Wilson's War."

Decorated in dark woods and rich burgundy hues, Chops evokes a '40s swing-era style, complete with Frank Sinatra and Dean Martin music, creating a "Rat Pack" ambience of a different age. Accented with oversized chairs, romantic lighting and touches of classic elegance, Chops steakhouse features premium cuts of quality steaks, fresh seafood, hearty side dishes and decadent desserts. Chops' open galley also allows our guests a direct view of the action behind the scene.

Chops Grille

You can choose to dine either in the elegant dining room or the cozy patio that opens into Central Park. Either way Chops Steakhouse is the perfect place for a romantic dinner or an encounter with friends.

Cured Seafood Trio

FISH

1 side fresh salmon,
center part only, boneless and skinless
1 side fresh halibut,
center part only, boneless and skinless
1 side fresh tuna,
center part only, boneless and skinless
10 star anise, crushed
1 bunch cilantro, finely chopped
1 bunch green onions, finely chopped
3 tablespoons (45 ml) extra virgin olive oil

CURE

1 pound (450 g) granulated sugar
1/4 pound (125 g) salt
3 teaspoons (45 ml) water

LEMON-GINGER VINAIGRETTE

1 tablespoon (15 ml) extra virgin olive oil
1 stalk lemongrass, chopped
1/2 teaspoon (2.5 g) finely chopped ginger
2 cloves garlic, peeled and finely chopped
Juice of 1 lemon
2 tablespoons (30 ml) rice vinegar
1/3 cup (90 ml) sweet chili sauce
2 tablespoons (30 ml) dark soy sauce
1/2 teaspoon (2.5 g) cornstarch
mixed in a little water
1 tablespoon (15 ml) freshly squeezed lime juice

AVOCADO SALAD

3 avocadoes, peeled and diced small
2 cucumbers, peeled, seeded and diced small
1/3 cup (85 g) wakame seaweed salad, store
bought
Juice of half lemon

GARNISH

6-ounces (170 g) micro greens
2-ounces (60 g) enoki mushrooms
1/2 red bell pepper, diced
1/2 green bell pepper, diced

EQUIPMENT

2 small glass or stainless steel bowls
Baking dish
Chef's knife and cutting board
Fine mesh strainer or Chinois
Pastry ring cutters
Plastic cling wrap
Sauté pan

Rub each fish fillet with crushed anise and press with cilantro and green onions.

Place sugar into a stainless steel or glass bowl, and gradually add salt, making sure flavor is balanced.

Transfer half of sugar mixture onto 3 plastic wrap sheets, top with fish fillets and cover with remaining sugar mixture. Drizzle with water and wrap tightly.

Place fish in baking dish and store in the refrigerator. Check the curing process of each fish every 2 hours. Salmon and tuna should cure for 4 hours. Halibut may need up to 6 hours.

Once cured, wash off sugar mixture under cold water, dry each fish thoroughly. Rub fish with olive oil and roll in plastic wrap to keep them moist. Keep refrigerated.

To make vinaigrette, in a small sauté pan over medium heat, warm oil and sauté lemongrass, ginger and garlic for 5 minutes. Add all remaining ingredients with the exception of the lime juice and simmer for 5 minutes. Thicken with cornstarch as necessary. Strain into a small glass bowl using a fine sieve and let cool. Mix in lime juice once cold.

Mix all ingredients for avocado salad into a small stainless steel bowl.

Distribute avocado salad into small pastry ring cutters, gently press with a spoon and transfer onto chilled plates.

Carve each fish into 1/2" thick slices and arrange in a fan next to the avocado salad.

Garnish with micro greens, enoki mushrooms and diced bell pepper and drizzle with lemon-ginger vinaigrette.

Serves 8.

Difficulty 5.

Beef Tenderloin and Eggplant Lover

LEMONGRASS OIL

2 stalks lemongrass, roughly cut
1 medium white onion, peeled and chopped
4 cloves garlic, peeled
1 bunch cilantro, roots only
1 medium size fresh gingerroot, peeled and roughly cut
1 cup (240 ml) vegetable oil

CILANTRO CHILI DRESSING

5 limes, peeled and cored
4 cloves garlic, peeled and chopped
2 shallots, peeled and chopped
1/4 cup (60 ml) fish sauce
2 tablespoons (60 g) palm sugar
1/4 cup (60 ml) soy sauce
1/2 teaspoon (2.5 g) Tom Yum paste
1/2 cup (120 ml) chicken stock (page 172)
1/2 bunch fresh cilantro, chopped
2 fresh jalapeños, deseeded and chopped

EGGPLANT

2 tablespoons (60 ml) extra virgin olive oil
1 medium eggplant, thinly sliced
Salt and freshly ground black pepper

BEEF

1 pound (450 g) beef tenderloin, tail end cut
2 tablespoons (60 ml) vegetable oil

SALAD

8-ounces (230 g) mesclun mix
4-ounces (115 g) baby watercress
2 Belgium endives, cut in half and julienned
1/4 bunch cilantro leaves
1/2 red bell pepper, julienned and kept in iced water
1/2 green bell pepper, julienned and kept in iced water
2 scallions, green part only, julienned
20 snow peas, blanched, julienned and kept in iced water

GARNISH

Parsley sprigs

EQUIPMENT

1 Chef's knife and cutting board
2 ovenproof baking dishes
Blender or hand mixer
Grill pan or heavy skillet
Large glass or stainless steel bowl
Medium size heavy saucepan
Small glass or stainless steel bowl
Small saucepan
Wire mesh strainer
Wire whisk

Preheat oven to 400°F or 205°C.

For lemongrass oil, place all ingredients into a small saucepan, cover and simmer for 30 minutes or until all ingredients reach a golden color.

Allow to cool and strain using a small sieve. Oil will keep for 2 weeks once refrigerated.

To make cilantro dressing, place all ingredients into a blender and purée. Pass though a sieve into a stainless steel or glass bowl and add 1/4 cup of lemongrass oil. Mix well and keep cool.

Liberally brush beef tenderloin with half of the cilantro-lemongrass mixture and marinate for 2 hours.

Lightly oil a grill pan and heat over medium-high heat. Place eggplant slices on grill and cook each side for 2 minutes, turning only once. Season with salt and pepper and transfer to a baking dish. Cook in the oven for 5 to 7 minutes or until eggplant is soft.

Remove eggplant from the oven and brush with lemongrass oil. Allow to cool.

Meanwhile, warm a grill pan over high heat and sear tenderloin on all sides. Transfer to an ovenproof dish and roast in the oven for 10 to 12 minutes or until medium rare.

Remove from oven, cover and let rest on the side of the stove for 10 minutes. Cut in 1/4" thick slices.

In a large stainless steel or glass bowl, toss all salad ingredients with remaining cilantro dressing.

Place two eggplant slices in the center of chilled plates, top with half of the salad mix and 2 beef slices, then the remaining salad and 2 more beef slices. Garnish with parsley sprigs and drizzle with additional lemongrass oil.

Serves 6.

Difficulty 3

Chops Salad

SALAD

12 baby beetroots, scrubbed clean
Salt and freshly ground black pepper
2 tablespoons (30 g) granulated sugar
2 tablespoons (30 g) unsalted butter
5-ounces (140 g) baby arugula lettuce
10-ounces (285 g) mesclun mix
4 plum tomatoes, washed and cut into wedges
8 hard boiled eggs, peeled and cut into wedges
12 strips bacon, baked until crisp
and cut into 1/2" pieces

VINAIGRETTE

1/2 cup (120 ml) extra virgin olive oil
8 shallots, peeled and halved
2 tablespoons (30 g) brown sugar
1/4 cup (60 ml) Cabernet wine
1/3 cup (90 ml) chicken stock (page 172)
1 teaspoon (15 g) Dijon mustard
1/4 cup (60 ml) red wine vinegar
Salt and freshly ground white pepper

GARNISH

Baby beetroot leaves

EQUIPMENT

Chef's knife and cutting board
Food processor or immersion blender
Medium sauté pan
Small glass or stainless steel bowl
Small sauté pan
Stockpot
Wire mesh strainer
Wire whisk

Place beetroots in a large pot filled with hot water and seasoned with salt. Bring to a boil and cook for 20 minutes or until beetroots are cooked through. Drain and refresh under cold water.

Peel beetroots with the back of a knife, cut into quarters, season with salt and pepper and sprinkle with sugar.

In a medium size sauté pan, melt butter over medium heat and sauté beetroots for 5 to 7 minutes or until caramelized.

For vinaigrette, in a small sauté pan over medium heat, warm 1 tablespoon olive oil and sauté shallots with brown sugar for 5 minutes. Deglaze with wine and reduce by half. Add chicken stock, bring to a boil, cover with aluminum foil and simmer for 15 minutes or until shallots are falling apart.

Strain liquid through a sieve and process shallots into a fine purée using a food processor. Combine liquid and shallot purée into a stainless steel or glass bowl and allow to cool.

Stir mustard into cooled shallot reduction, add vinegar and whisk in remaining olive oil. Adjust seasoning with salt and pepper.

Assemble lettuces on chilled plates. Garnish with tomatoes, eggs, bacon and baby caramelized beetroots. Drizzle with shallot vinaigrette and decorate with baby beetroot leaves.

Serves 8.

Difficulty 2.

Forest Mushroom Soup

SOUP

3 tablespoons (45 ml) extra virgin olive oil
1 clove garlic, peeled and chopped
2 medium yellow onions, peeled and diced
10-ounces (485 g) crimini mushrooms
10-ounces (485 g) button mushrooms
10-ounces (485 g) small portabella
  mushrooms or 2 large mushrooms
2 large Idaho potatoes,
  peeled and thickly sliced
1 sprig thyme
1 bay leaf
1/2 cup (120 ml) dry white wine
1 quart (1 L) vegetable stock (page 172)
Salt and freshly ground black pepper
1/4 cup (60 ml) heavy cream

GARNISH

4-ounces (120 g) enoki mushrooms
3 tablespoons (45 ml) white truffle oil

EQUIPMENT

2 large saucepans or medium size stockpots
Chef's knife and cutting board
Food processor or immersion blender
Ladle
Wooden spoon

In a large saucepan or medium size stockpot, over medium heat, warm oil and sauté garlic and onions for 4 minutes.

Add mushrooms, potatoes and herbs and sauté for 5 minutes, allowing potatoes to begin to caramelize.

Deglaze with white wine and add vegetable stock. Bring to a boil and simmer for 10 minutes or until potatoes are soft to the touch. Season with salt and pepper.

In batches, transfer mixture into a food processor and blend until smooth. Pour into a clean saucepan, add heavy cream and mix well. Taste, adjust seasoning if necessary and keep warm.

Ladle soup into warmed bowls, garnish with enoki mushrooms and a drizzle of truffle oil.

Serves 6.

Difficulty 1.

Dirty Martini

2 oz (6 cl) vodka or gin
1/4 oz (0.75 cl) dry vermouth
1/4 oz (0.75 cl) olive juice

Garnish
Small skewer
4 pitted green olives

Fill a cocktail shaker with ice. Pour all ingredients into shaker. Shake well and strain into a chilled martini glass. Garnish with an olive skewer.

Chops Grille

Herb Crusted Jumbo Shrimp

BEURRE BLANC

1 tablespoon (15 ml) vegetable oil
1 small white onion, peeled and minced
2 tablespoons (30 ml) white wine
1 tablespoon (15 ml) white wine vinegar
1/4 cup (60 ml) fish stock (page 172)
1/4 cup (60 ml) clam juice
1/4 cup (60 ml) heavy cream, reduced by half
1/2 pound (250 g) unsalted butter, cubed
2-ounces (60 g) lump crab meat, crumbled
Juice of 1 lime
Salt and freshly ground white pepper

CRUST

3/4 cup (175 g) butter, room temperature
1/4 cup (60 g) margarine, room temperature
1 bunch cilantro, chopped
1/4 cup (60 g) finely chopped garlic
3 tablespoons (45 g) finely chopped ginger
1 egg
1 egg yolk
1 cup (235 g) Panko breadcrumbs
Salt and freshly ground white pepper

SHRIMP

12 extra large size shrimp, peeled, deveined,
tails left on and butterflied (size U4)

VEGETABLES

1 tablespoon (15 ml) extra virgin olive oil
24 cherry tomatoes, halved
2 tablespoons (30 g) butter
24 green asparagus, peeled, blanched
and refreshed in ice water
Salt and freshly ground black pepper

GARNISH

1 green onion, halved and julienned
3 limes

EQUIPMENT

9" x 13" baking dish or medium sheet pan
Chef's knife and cutting board
Large glass or stainless steel bowl
Large sauté pan
Medium sauté pan
Rubber spatula
Small sauté pan
Stand mixer or hand mixer
Wire mesh strainer or Chinois
Wire whisk
Wooden spoon

Preheat oven to 450°F or 205°C.

For beurre blanc, in a small sauté pan over medium heat, warm oil and sauté onion for 3 minutes or until translucent. Deglaze with white wine. Add vinegar, fish stock and clam juice, bring to a boil and simmer for 10 minutes or until reduced by half. Add cream and strain through a fine sieve.

Adjust seasoning with salt and pepper. Whisk in butter and fold in crab meat and lime juice. Keep warm by placing in a small glass bowl in a bain marie.

In a large glass or stainless steel bowl, join butter and margarine and whip using a hand mixer at medium speed until it has doubled in volume. Add cilantro, garlic and ginger and mix well. Fold in eggs and breadcrumbs and season with salt and pepper.

Arrange shrimp on a baking sheet pan and evenly coat with butter mixture. Bake for 6 minutes.

For tomatoes, in a medium sauté pan over medium heat, warm oil and sauté tomatoes for 2 minutes. Season with salt and pepper.

For asparagus, in a large sauté pan over medium heat, melt butter and sauté for 3 minutes, or until warm. Season with salt and pepper.

Place asparagus off center in warmed plates and top with shrimp. Surround with tomatoes and drizzle with crab beurre blanc. Garnish with julienned green onion and lime slices.

Serves 6.

Difficulty 2.

WINE PAIRING ◇ DOMAINE DENIS GAUDRY, POUILLY-FUMÉ, LOIRE, FRANCE

WINE PAIRING ⌒ MERLOT, RUBICON ESTATE, NAPA, CALIFORNIA

Beef Short Ribs

SHORT RIBS

8 beef short ribs, bone-in
Salt and freshly ground black pepper
¼ cup (60 ml) extra virgin olive oil
1 large yellow onion, peeled and chopped
2 stalks celery, chopped
2 carrots, peeled and chopped
1 750-ml bottle Cabernet wine
1 ½ quarts (1.4 L) veal or
    beef stock (page 173)

MASHED POTATOES

2 pounds (900 g) Yukon Gold potatoes,
    peeled and quartered
¾ cup (175 ml) heavy cream
2 tablespoons (30 g) unsalted butter
Salt and freshly ground white pepper

GRILLED TOMATOES

4 Roma tomatoes, halved
2 tablespoons (30 ml) extra virgin olive oil
Salt and freshly ground black pepper

BROCCOLINI

1 tablespoon (15 g) butter
1 bunch broccolini, trimmed or 1 head broccoli,
    cut into florets, steamed and refreshed in
    ice water
Salt and freshly ground black pepper

GARNISH

Baby watercress

EQUIPMENT

Baking dish
Chef's knife and cutting board
Ladle
Large sauté pan
Metal tongs
Ovenproof baking dish or Dutch oven
Potato ricer
Small sauté pan
Stockpot

Preheat oven to 350°F or 180°C.

Season ribs with salt and pepper.

In a large, heavy bottomed ovenproof pan over high heat, warm oil and brown ribs, in batches, on all sides. Transfer ribs to a plate as you work.

Using the same pan, reduce heat to medium and sauté onions, celery and carrots for 5 minutes. Pour off excess fat and deglaze with wine, scraping any bits from the bottom of the pan.

Reduce wine for 15 minutes or until thick and syrupy in consistency.

Return ribs to pan and add stock and enough water to cover the ribs. Bring to a boil, cover and braise in the oven for 2 to 2 ½ hours or until meat is tender and easily separates from the bone. Allow ribs to cool in the liquid. Cover and refrigerate overnight.

The next day, remove solidified excess fat and return to medium heat, uncovered. Cook for 1 hour or until liquid has reduced by three quarters, frequently spooning sauce over ribs to keep them moist.

For mashed potatoes, place potatoes into salted cold water, bring to a boil and cook until potatoes are easily pierced with the tip of a knife, about 15 minutes. Drain and press potatoes through a potato ricer into a heated bowl. Stir in cream and butter. Adjust seasoning with salt and pepper. Set aside and keep warm.

Drizzle tomatoes with olive oil and season with salt and pepper. Using a small sauté pan over high heat, mark each tomato half and transfer into a small sheet pan. Finish cooking in the oven for 10 minutes.

For broccolini, in a large sauté pan over medium heat, melt butter and sauté vegetables for 3 minutes, or until warm. Season with salt and pepper.

Arrange a spoonful of mashed potatoes in the center of warmed plates. Top with a short rib and garnish with watercress sprig. Complement each plate with a grilled tomato, broccolini florets and a drizzle of sauce.

Serves 8.

Difficulty 4.

Granny's Caramel Apple Tart

CRÈME ANGLAISE

2 egg yolks
1/4 cup (60 g) sugar
1 cup (250 ml) milk
1 vanilla pod, split lengthwise

CRUST

1 cup (235 g) all-purpose flour
1/2 cup (115 g) graham crackers, crumbled
1/2 cup (115 g) granulated sugar
3/4 cup (175 g) unsalted butter, softened

Or

1 pie crust, store bought

FILLING

6 green apples, peeled, cored,
    sliced and quartered
1/3 cup (85 g) raisins
2 tablespoons (30 g) granulated sugar
1 teaspoon (5 g) cinnamon powder
1 cup (235 g) yellow cake crumbs

CRUMBLE

1 1/2 cups (370 g) all-purpose flour
1 cup (250 g) granulated sugar
1/2 cup (120 g) unsalted butter, room
    temperature

CARAMEL

1 cup (235 g) granulated sugar
1/2 cup (120 ml) water
1/2 cup (120 ml) heavy cream

Vanilla ice cream

GARNISH

8 dried apple slices, store bought

EQUIPMENT

13 x 9 x 4-inch (33 x 22 x 10 cm)
    baking pan
2 medium stainless steel bowls
Chef's knife and cutting board
Large glass or stainless steel bowl
Medium heavy saucepan
Mixing spoon
Small glass or stainless steel bowl
Small saucepan
Spatula and wooden spoon
Stand mixer with paddle
    attachment or hand mixer
Wire whisk

Preheat oven to 350°F or 180°C.

Prepare crème anglaise by creaming egg yolks with sugar in a glass bowl. Bring milk and vanilla pods to a boil and slowly simmer for about 10 minutes or until cream coats the back of a wooden spoon. Do not allow sauce to boil. Remove from heat and pour into a small glass or stainless steel bowl. Place crème-filled bowl in a large bowl filled with ice and water. Stir to cool. Discard vanilla pod, cover and refrigerate.

For pie, grease a baking pan and set aside.
To make the crust, combine all ingredients in the large bowl of an electric mixer and mix on low speed until mixture is crumbly. Press mixture evenly into greased baking pan.

Bake 20 minutes and remove from oven.

Meanwhile, in a medium size glass or stainless steel bowl, combine apple slices, raisins, sugar, cinnamon and cake crumbs, then press out onto par-cooked crust.

Make crumbles by hand-mixing all ingredients in a glass bowl until crumbles form. Sprinkle over apple mixture.
Bake for 20 minutes or until apples are soft and crumbles are golden brown.

For caramel, melt sugar and water in a small saucepan over medium heat and simmer until golden brown. Remove from heat and slowly whisk in cream.

Serve slices of warm apple tart drizzled with caramel sauce and topped with a scoop of vanilla ice cream.
Garnish with a dried apple slice and a spoonful of crème anglaise.

Serves 8.
Difficulty 4.

Bailey's Chocolate Café

1 1/2 oz (4.5 cl) Bailey's Irish Cream
1/4 oz (0.75 cl) espresso
1/2 oz (1.5 cl) vodka
1/2 oz (1.5 cl) white crème de cocoa
1/4 oz (0.75 cl) Frangelico
1 oz (3 cl) half & half

Fill shaker with ice and add all ingredients. Shake well and pour into a rock glass.

Marco Marrama, Senior Executive Chef

NORTHERN ITALY, INFLUENCED BY THE LUXURIOUS RIVIERA, GIVES OUR PORTOFINO RESTAURANT ITS INSPIRATION.

CRISP LINENS, SOFT LIGHTING, ORNATE ITALIAN CERAMICS, AND OF COURSE, THE AZURE OCEAN BEYOND THE WINDOWS ... ALL ACCENTED WITH SOFT ARIAS IN THE BACKGROUND.

IT'S LIKE DINING IN ONE OF THE CASTLES ABOVE PORTOFINO BAY WHILE SIPPING A BELINI. AND THE CUISINE, AHHH!

CONTEMPORARY INSALATA DI PETTO DI ANATRA AFFUMICATA. CLASSIC OSSOBUCCO ALLA PIEMONTESE. OR SCRUMPTIOUS DOLCETTI ALLA PORTOFINO SERVED BY A DISCREET AND DISTINGUISHED WAIT STAFF WILL MAKE YOUR TASTE BUDS SING WITH ENJOYMENT.

BELLISIMA!

Portofino

Insalata di Petto di Anatra Affumicata

(Sliced Smoked Duck Over Arugula and Field Mushroom Confit)

GARLIC CONFIT

1 head of garlic, peeled and shaved
1/3 cup (90 ml) extra virgin olive oil

SALAD

1 tablespoon (15 ml) extra virgin olive oil
7-ounces (200 g) crimini mushrooms, quartered
5-ounces (140 g) portabella mushrooms, sliced
7-ounces (200 g) button mushrooms, quartered
Salt and freshly ground white pepper

6-ounces (170 g) arugula
3/4 pound (375 g) smoked duck, sliced
12 green asparagus, peeled,
   blanched and refreshed in iced water
Parmesan shavings

1/2 cup (115 g) cherry tomatoes, halved
1 tablespoon (15 ml) white truffle oil

EQUIPMENT

Baking dish
Chef's knife and cutting board
Sauté pan
Small saucepan
Wooden spoon

In a small saucepan over medium heat, simmer garlic in olive oil for 20 minutes. Do not brown. Remove from heat and cover.

In a sauté pan over medium heat, warm oil and sauté mushrooms for 2 minutes. Season with salt and pepper and transfer into a small baking dish. Cover with garlic confit and allow cooling.

Position mushrooms in the center of chilled plates, making sure the least amount of garlic confit gets on the plates, crest with arugula, smoked duck slices, asparagus and Parmesan shavings. Garnish with cherry tomatoes and drizzle with truffle oil.

Serves 6.

Difficulty 1.

Portofino

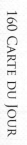

Risotto ai Gamberetti

RISOTTO

3 tablespoons (45 ml) extra virgin olive oil
2 shallots, small diced
1 clove garlic, minced
2 cups (465 g) Arborio rice
1/4 teaspoon (1 g) saffron threads
1/4 cup (60 ml) dry white wine
6 cups (1.4 L) fish or vegetable stock, simmering (page 172)
2 tablespoons (30 g) butter
1/3 cup (90 ml) heavy cream
1/3 cup (85 g) freshly grated Parmesan cheese
Salt and freshly ground white pepper

SHRIMP

4 tablespoons (60 g) butter
18 pieces large shrimp (size 16/20), raw, peeled and deveined
1/4 cup (60 ml) dry white wine
1 tablespoon (15 g) lobster base, purchased
1/4 cup (60 ml) water

GARNISH

1/4 bunch parsley, finely chopped
1 onion, thinly sliced, lightly floured and fried

EQUIPMENT

Chef's knife and cutting board
Fine mesh strainer or Chinois
Ladle
Large saucepan
Large sauté pan
Medium saucepan
Slotted spoon
Wire whisk
Wooden spoon

In a large saucepan over medium heat, warm oil and sauté shallots and garlic for 4 minutes. Add rice and stir until each grain is well coated with oil, about 3 minutes. Add saffron and wine and stir until liquid is completely absorbed.

Add stock to rice a ladleful at a time, stirring frequently after each addition. Make sure rice never gets dry. Season with salt and pepper.

When the rice is tender to the bite, after about 20 minutes, add butter, heavy cream and Parmesan cheese and mix well. Set aside and keep warm.

For shrimp, in a sauté pan over medium heat, melt butter and sauté shrimp for 2 minutes on each side. Deglaze with white wine, stir in lobster base and water and simmer for 5 minutes.

Remove shrimp from sauce and pass through a sieve. Whisk butter into sauce a little at a time.

Arrange risotto in warmed appetizer plates and top with 3 shrimp. Drizzle with sauce and garnish with chopped parsley and fried onions.

Serves 6.

Difficulty 3.

Penne alla Caminetto

GARLIC CONFIT

1 head of garlic, peeled and shaved
1/3 cup (90 ml) extra virgin olive oil

SAUCE

2 medium yellow onions, diced
2 carrots, finely chopped
2 celery stalks, finely chopped
1 2-ounce (60 g) slice prosciutto ham, small diced, soaked in warm water
4-ounces (120 g) dry porcini mushrooms, soaked in water and julienned
3/4 pound (375 g) beef strips
1/2 cup (120 ml) Chardonnay wine
1 (15-ounce) (450 g) can stripped Italian tomatoes with juice
Salt and freshly ground black pepper
2 plum tomatoes, peeled, seeded and chopped
2 tablespoons (30 g) chopped parsley
1 1/2 pounds (700 g) dry penne pasta
1 teaspoon (5 ml) extra virgin olive oil

GARNISH

Parmesan shavings
Parsley sprigs

EQUIPMENT

Chef's knife and cutting board
Large sauté pan
Slotted spoon
Small saucepan
Stockpot or large pot
Wooden spoon

In a small saucepan over medium heat, simmer garlic in olive oil for 20 minutes. Do not brown. Allow to cool. Cover and reserve.

To make sauce, in a skillet over medium heat, warm 3 tablespoons (45 ml) garlic confit and sauté onions, carrots and celery for 6 to 8 minutes or until vegetables reach a light golden color. Add prosciutto and porcini mushrooms (reserve soaking water for future use) and sauté for 3 minutes. Add beef and cook for 5 minutes. Deglaze with white wine, add strained porcini water and canned tomatoes, season with salt and pepper, bring to a boil and simmer for 1 hour, stirring occasionally.

While sauce is simmering, cook penne pasta in a stockpot of boiling salted water until al dente, about 10 to 12 minutes. Drain well and toss with olive oil.

Finish sauce by adding the chopped plum tomatoes and parsley.

Add pasta to sauce. Toss to coat and arrange in warmed pasta bowls. Garnish with Parmesan shavings and parsley sprigs.

Serves 6.

Difficulty 2.

WINE PAIRING ⤳ BARONS DE ROTHSCHILD - LAFITE, PAUILLAC, "RÉSERVE SPÉCIALE", FRANCE

Wine Pairing ☙ Chardonnay, Cabreo, Toscana, "La Pietra", Italy

Spiedino di Frutti di Mare alla Toscana

(Tuscan Seafood Brochette)

MARINADE

1/4 cup (60 ml) extra virgin olive oil
3 cloves garlic, shaved
1 teaspoon (5 g) fresh thyme
2 tablespoons (30 g) julienned basil
2 tablespoons (30 g) chopped parsley

SEAFOOD SKEWER

3 (6 to 7-ounce) (170 to 200 g) lobster tails,
    cut in half and deveined
12 large size shrimp, peeled,
    deveined, and tails on (size 16/20)
12 sea scallops (size 10/20)
1 1/2 pounds (700 g) salmon, cubed large
Salt and freshly ground black pepper

6 long skewers (18-inch or 45 cm)

MARINARA SAUCE

1/2 tablespoon (7.5 g) pine nuts
1/2 tablespoon (7.5 ml) extra virgin olive oil
1/2 onion, diced
1 clove garlic, chopped
3 ripe tomatoes, peeled, seeded and diced
1/4 teaspoon (1 g) chopped basil
Salt and freshly ground black pepper
1/2 tablespoon (7.5 ml) balsamic vinegar

SUNDRIED TOMATO BEURRE BLANC

1 teaspoon (5 ml) extra virgin olive oil
2 shallots, minced
1 small onion, diced
6 black peppercorns, crushed
1/4 cup (60 ml) dry white wine
1/2 cup (120 ml) fish stock (page 172)
2 tablespoons (30 ml) white wine vinegar
1/4 cup (60 ml) heavy cream
5 sundried tomatoes, sliced
1 pound (450 g) unsalted butter, room
    temperature
Salt and freshly ground white pepper

LIGURIAN POTATOES

2 pounds (1 kg) Idaho potatoes,
    peeled and thickly sliced
1 cup (250 ml) vegetable oil
1 tablespoon (15 ml) garlic oil (purchased)
1 tablespoon (15 ml) onion oil (purchased)
Salt and freshly ground black pepper

1/4 cup (60 g) pine nuts, toasted

VEGETABLES

12 fresh green asparagus, trimmed
12 baby squash
6 baby zucchini, cut diagonally

EQUIPMENT

2 large sauté pans
6 bamboo skewers
Baking sheet
Chef's knife and cutting board
Colander
Food processor or blender
Medium saucepan
Outdoor grill or grill pan
Paper towels
Small glass or stainless steel bowl
Small saucepan
Wire mesh strainer or Chinois
Wire whisk
Wooden spoon

Preheat oven to 350°F or 180°C.

In a small bowl, mix all ingredients for marinade. Rub into fish and seafood. Thread the fish and seafood through their center on thin skewers. Cover and refrigerate for 1 hour.

For marinara, place pine nuts on a baking sheet in the oven for 2 minutes or until pine nuts are golden brown.

In a small saucepan over medium heat, warm oil and sauté onion for 4 minutes or until translucent. Add garlic and sauté for 1 minute, stirring continually. Do not brown. Add tomatoes and herbs and season with salt and pepper. Cover and simmer for 10 minutes. Add vinegar and 3/4 of the pine nuts, season to taste, stir gently and set aside.

To prepare beurre blanc, in a saucepan over medium heat, warm oil and sauté shallots and onions for 4 minutes. Add crushed peppercorns and deglaze with white wine.

Add fish stock and white wine vinegar. Bring to a simmer and slowly reduce liquid by half. Add cream and

sundried tomatoes and simmer for 10 minutes or until sauce coats the back of a wooden spoon. Do not boil. Blend and strain through a fine sieve and whisk in butter a little at a time. Season with salt and pepper. Set aside.

For Ligurian potatoes, blanch potatoes in cold salted water. Bring to a boil and cook for 10 minutes. Cool in cold water, drain and pan-fry in hot oil for 5 to 7 minutes or until potatoes are golden and crispy to the touch. Transfer on paper towels to absorb excess fat.

In a sauté pan over medium heat, warm garlic and onion oils, add fried potatoes and sauté for 2 minutes. Add toasted pine nuts and enough marinara sauce to coat potatoes. Drizzle with balsamic vinegar and adjust seasoning with salt and pepper. Keep warm.

To grill seafood:

Outdoor grill: Heat to medium-high heat. Place skewers on grill and cook each side for 2 to 4 minutes, turning

only once. Season with salt and pepper. Remove from grill and finish in oven for 5 minutes.

Indoor grill: Lightly oil a grill pan. Set temperature to medium-high heat. Place skewers on grill and cook each side for 2 to 4 minutes, turning only once. Season with salt and pepper. Remove from grill and finish in oven for 5 minutes.

Separately blanch asparagus, baby squash and zucchini in boiling salted water for 3 minutes. Keep warm.

Place skewer on warmed plate alongside potatoes and vegetables.

Serve sundried tomato beurre blanc on the side.

Serves 6.

Difficulty 4.

Saltimbocca alla Romana

(Veal Saltimbocca Romana)

VEAL SCALOPPINE

12 veal scaloppine,
1 1/2 to 2 inches (5 cm) thick
Salt and freshly ground black pepper
12 sage leaves
12 prosciutto slices, thin
1/2 cup (120 g) flour
6 tablespoons (85 g) clarified unsalted butter
1/4 cup (60 ml) Marsala
1 cup (250 ml) dry white wine
2 cups (500 ml) veal demi-glace (page 173)
1 tablespoon (15 g) unsalted butter

RISOTTO

1/3 cup (90 g) dried porcini mushrooms
7-8 cups (1.5 to 2 L) chicken or vegetable
stock (page 172)
1/4 cup (60 ml) extra virgin olive oil
2 shallots, finely chopped
1 clove garlic, chopped
3 cups (750 g) Arborio rice
1/2 cup (120 ml) dry white wine
Salt and freshly ground white pepper
2 tablespoons (30 g) unsalted butter
1/4 cup (60 g) Parmesan cheese, freshly grated

1 tablespoon (15 ml) extra virgin olive oil
1/3 cup (100 g) fresh crimini mushrooms,
thickly sliced

Salt and freshly ground black pepper
12 baby zucchini, halved lengthwise
1 tablespoon (15 ml) extra virgin olive oil

GARNISH

Fresh sage leaves

EQUIPMENT

Grill pan
Ladle
Large saucepan
Mallet
Medium saucepan
Metal tongs
Plastic wrap
Skillet
Small saucepans
Wire mesh strainer or Chinois
Wire whisk
Wooden spoon

Flatten the veal fairly thin with the flat side of a mallet.
Season with salt and black pepper, then place a fresh sage
leaf and prosciutto on top of each scaloppine. To keep
the prosciutto in place during cooking, place the meat
between layers of plastic wrap and pound gently with the
flat side of the mallet.

Dredge meat in flour. Shake off any excess.

Heat clarified unsalted butter in a large skillet and sauté
veal for 1 minute on each side, starting with ham side
down. Remove from pan and keep warm.

Using the same pan, add Marsala, then the wine and
reduce slightly. Add veal demi-glace and reduce by half.
Remove from heat. Strain into a small saucepan and whisk
in butter. Keep warm.

For risotto, place dried mushrooms in warm water for
15 minutes.

In a saucepan over medium heat, bring stock to a simmer
and maintain over low heat.

In a large saucepan, heat olive oil over medium heat.
Add shallots and garlic and sauté until translucent, about
4 minutes. Add dried mushrooms and rice and stir until
each grain is well coated with oil, about 3 minutes. Add
wine and stir until it is completely absorbed. Add stock
to rice a ladleful at a time, stirring frequently after each
addition until absorbed. Make sure the rice never gets
dry. Season with salt and white pepper.

When rice is tender, about 20 minutes, add butter and
grated cheese. Set aside.

Over medium heat, in a small saucepan, warm olive oil
and sauté crimini mushrooms for 3 minutes.

Finish risotto by adding a ladle of stock and the sautéed
mushrooms to rice. Warm up over low heat for 2 minutes.

Season zucchini and rub with olive oil. Heat a grilling pan
over medium heat and grill for five minutes, turning once.

Serve risotto on a warmed plate, topped with veal.
Garnish with grilled zucchini and a spoonful of Marsala
reduction.

Serves 6.

Difficulty 5.

WINE PAIRING ⌘ L'ECOLE NO. 41, SYRAH, "SEVEN HILLS VINEYARD", WALLA WALLA, WASHINGTON

WINE PAIRING ❧ CAPOSALDO, PROSECCO, BRUT, VENETO, ITALY

Dolcetti alla Portofino (pages 168-170)

Tiramisù

TIRAMISÙ
3 egg yolks
2 tablespoons (30 g) sugar
3/4 cup (150 g) mascarpone cheese at room temperature
2 tablespoons (30 ml) amaretto
1/4 cup (60 ml) heavy cream
3 egg whites
2 tablespoons (30 g) sugar
1 leaf of gelatin (purchased)
1/4 cup (60 ml) lukewarm water
3 tablespoons (45 ml) Kahlúa®
3 tablespoons (45 ml) espresso coffee or strong brewed coffee
8 ladyfingers

GARNISH
Cocoa powder, for dusting

EQUIPMENT
5 medium glass or stainless steel bowls
Hand mixer
Medium saucepan
Rubber spatula
Wire whisk
Wooden spoon

In a medium bowl mix egg yolks and sugar; blanch using an electric mixer at high speed for about 5 minutes or until mixture is frothy. Place bowl over a pot of simmering water and whisk, at medium speed for 10 more minutes or until mixture has doubled in volume. Remove from heat.

In a bowl, break up mascarpone, add amaretto, and whisk until well blended.

In a chilled mixing bowl, whip heavy cream into stiff peaks and fold into mascarpone mixture.

Beat egg whites with sugar until stiff.

Soften gelatin in water. Remove from water and slowly fold into the lukewarm egg yolk mixture. Gently fold egg yolks and mascarpone mixtures into egg whites.

In a separate bowl, mix Kahlúa® and espresso coffee. Cut ladyfingers in half, across, and soak in espresso mixture.

Place 2 pieces of soaked ladyfingers in the bottom of shot glasses and top with mascarpone cream. Chill for 2 hours or until set.

To serve, dust tiramisù cups with cocoa powder.

Serves 8.

Difficulty 5.

Flourless Chocolate Cake

3/4 cup (150 g) semisweet chocolate chips
3/4 cup (150 g) unsalted butter
4 eggs
1/2 cup (120 g) sugar
1 tablespoon (15 ml) dark rum
1/2 tablespoon (7.5 ml) vanilla extract
1/3 cup (90 ml) strong brewed coffee

CHOCOLATE WAFFLES
3/4 cup (150 g) semisweet chocolate chips
Bubble wrap

GARNISH
Whipped cream

EQUIPMENT
2 medium glass or stainless steel bowls
8-inch (20-cm) pan or 8 molds
Aluminum foil
Hand mixer
Medium saucepan
Roasting pan or baking dish
Rubber spatula
Wire rack
Wire whisk
Wooden spoon

Preheat oven to 300°F or 150°C.

Place chocolate and butter in the top of a double boiler set over 1 inch (2.5 cm) of simmering water. Whisk until chocolate is smooth. Set aside to cool, stirring continuously.

Using an electric mixer, beat eggs and sugar until creamy. Gradually fold chocolate into egg mixture, add rum, vanilla extract and coffee and mix well.

Bring a large kettle of water to a boil.

Pour mixture into prepared 8-inch (20-cm) pan or 8 individual molds and cover with aluminum foil. Place in a roasting pan and pour in enough boiling water to come halfway up the outside of the pan. Bake for 30 minutes or until a skewer inserted comes out clean.

Remove cake(s) from oven and allow cooling to room temperature in pan. Transfer to a wire rack and chill overnight.

For chocolate waffles, place chocolate in the top of a double boiler set over 1 inch (2.5 cm) of simmering water. Whisk until chocolate is smooth. Spread over bubble wrap and allow to cool. Refrigerate for 1 hour. Remove bubble wrap and cut into triangles.

Cut cake as desired if necessary. Pipe a rosette of whipped cream atop each cake and garnish with a chocolate waffle.

Serves 8.

Difficulty 5.

Dolcetti alla Portofino

Panna Cotta

EQUIPMENT
8 ramekins or individual molds
Hand mixer
Medium glass or stainless steel bowl
Saucepan
Small glass bowl
Wooden spoon

1 gelatin leaf (purchased)
1/4 cup (60 g) strawberry jelly
4 egg whites
1 cup (250 ml) milk
2 cups (450 ml) heavy cream
1/4 cup (60 g) sugar
2 tablespoons (30 g) powdered pistachio

GARNISH
Unsalted pistachios, chopped

Place gelatin leaf in a bowl of warm water to soften. Layer bottom of ramekins with strawberry jelly. In a medium bowl, using an electric mixer, whisk egg whites until soft peaks form.

In a saucepan, over low heat, warm milk, cream, sugar and pistachio.

Remove from heat and fold in softened gelatin. Cool, stirring constantly, for 5 to 7 minutes. Gently mix with egg white mixture and pour into individual molds. Refrigerate for 3 hours.

Upon serving, remove from molds and garnish with pistachios.

Serves 8.

Difficulty 5.

White Chocolate Pot de Crème

EQUIPMENT
Medium glass or stainless steel bowl
Medium saucepan
Shallow pan or baking dish
Wire whisk

1/4 cup (60 g) white chocolate chips
2 eggs
1/4 cup (60 g) sugar
1 cup (250 ml) milk

GARNISH
Mint leaves
Chocolate sticks, purchased
Chocolate triangles, purchased

Preheat oven to 300°F or 150°C. Place chocolate in the top of a double boiler set over 1 inch (2.5 cm) of simmering water. Whisk until chocolate is smooth.

Prepare crème by creaming eggs with sugar. Bring milk to a boil and slowly stir into egg mixture. Add melted chocolate and pour mixture into individual molds set in a shallow pan

or baking dish. Cover with aluminum foil. Pour hot water into pan until it is halfway up the sides of the molds and bake for 20 minutes. Refrigerate for 2 hours.

Garnish with a chocolate stick and a chocolate triangle. Finish with mint leaves.

Serves 8.

Difficulty 5.

Limoncello Tartini

1 oz (3 cl) vodka
1/2 oz (1.5 cl) Limoncello
1/2 oz (1.5 cl) Sweet & Sour mix
1/2 oz (1.5 cl) vanilla syrup

Fill shaker with ice and add all ingredients. Shake well and strain into an ice filled rock glass. Garnish with a lemon wedge.

Aperol Fizz

1 1/2 oz (4.5 cl) Aperol
1 1/2 oz (4.5 cl) dry white wine
3 oz (9 cl) sparkling water

Fill cocktail shaker with ice. Pour all ingredients into the shaker and stir. Pour into a rock glass and garnish with an orange wheel and a pitted green olive.

Portofino

Cooking Basics

Chicken Stock

5 pounds (2.25 kg) chicken bones, including feet and neck, or 2 roasted chicken carcasses

3 quarts (2.8 L) cold water

2 carrots, peeled and coarsely sliced

2 medium onions, coarsely chopped

2 stalks celery, coarsely chopped

1 leek, washed and cut into 1/2-inch (1.2 cm) chunks

2 cloves garlic, crushed

2 bay leaves

3 parsley sprigs

1/4 teaspoon (1.5 g) black peppercorns

Place chicken bones into a large pot and pour in cold water to cover by 2 inches (5 cm). Bring to a boil, regularly skimming off fat and froth that rise to the surface.

Once water is boiling, add remaining ingredients, reduce heat to low, cover and simmer for 2 1/2 to 3 hours, skimming occasionally.

Strain stock through a fine sieve lined with several layers of cheesecloth and refrigerate, uncovered, overnight.

Discard congealed layer of fat on the surface and strain once again into small containers or ice cube trays.

Use stock immediately or freeze it and use as needed.

Makes 2 1/2 quarts (2.4 L).

Fish Stock

BOUQUET GARNI

3 sprigs parsley

3 celery leaves

1 sprig thyme

1/4 teaspoon (1.5 g) black peppercorns

1 bay leaf

STOCK

2 tablespoons (30 ml) extra virgin olive oil

1 pound (450 g) fish bones and heads from any saltwater fish, except salmon

1 carrot, peeled and coarsely sliced

1 shallot, coarsely chopped

1 small onion, coarsely chopped

1 stalk celery, coarsely chopped

1 clove garlic, crushed

1 leek, washed and cut into 1/2-inch (1.2 cm) chunks

1/4 cup (60 ml) dry white wine

5 cups (1.2 L) cold water

Prepare bouquet garni by wrapping parsley, celery, thyme, peppercorns and bay leaf inside a piece of cheesecloth and tying it with kitchen string.

In a saucepan over medium heat, warm oil and sauté fish bones and vegetables for 8 minutes. Add wine and stir, scraping the bottom of the pan. Add bouquet garni and enough water to completely cover fish. Bring to a boil, regularly skimming off fat and froth that rise to the surface. Reduce heat to low and simmer for 30 minutes.

Strain stock through a fine sieve lined with several layers of cheesecloth.

Use stock immediately or freeze it in small containers and use as needed.

Makes 1 quart (950 ml).

Vegetable Stock

2 tablespoons (30 ml) extra virgin olive oil

1 medium onion, coarsely chopped

1 leek, washed and cut into 1/2-inch (1.2 cm) chunks

1 stalk celery, coarsely chopped

1 turnip, peeled and coarsely chopped

2 carrots, peeled and coarsely chopped

2 tomatoes, peeled, seeded and chopped

1 clove garlic, crushed

3 sprigs parsley

1 sprig thyme

1 bay leaf

1/4 teaspoon (1.5 g) black peppercorns

5 cups (1.2 L) cold water

Heat oil in a stockpot over medium heat. Add vegetables and sauté for 10 minutes. Do not brown.

Add enough water to completely cover the vegetables. Reduce heat to low and simmer for 30 minutes.

Strain stock through a fine sieve lined with several layers of cheesecloth.

Use immediately or freeze it into small containers and use as needed.

Makes 1 quart (950 ml).

Beef Stock

4 pounds (1.8 kg) beef bones
1/2 pound (250 g) veal trimmings
1 onion, coarsely chopped
2 carrots, peeled and coarsely chopped
2 stalks celery, coarsely chopped
1 leek, washed and cut into 1/2-inch (1.2 cm) chunks
1 tablespoon (15 g) tomato paste
2 bay leaves
3 parsley sprigs
1/4 teaspoon (1.5 g) black peppercorns
2 1/2 quarts (2.4 L) cold water

Preheat oven to 400°F or 200°C.

Place beef bones, veal trimmings and onion in a roasting pan and roast uncovered for 1 hour or until bones are golden brown.

Transfer to a stockpot. Add remaining ingredients and pour in enough water to cover completely. Bring to a boil, uncovered, over medium heat. Reduce heat to low and simmer for 8 to 10 hours. Set aside and let cool.

Strain through a fine sieve lined with several layers of cheesecloth.

Use immediately or freeze it in small containers and use as needed.

Makes 2 quarts (1.8 L).

Brown Sauce

BOUQUET GARNI
3 sprigs parsley
3 celery leaves
1 sprig thyme
1/4 teaspoon (1.5 g) black peppercorns
1 bay leaf

SAUCE
4 tablespoons (60 g) unsalted butter
2 medium onions, diced
3 carrots, peeled and diced
3 stalks celery, diced
1/3 cup (90 g) all-purpose flour
3 tablespoons (45 g) tomato paste
4 cups (950 ml) beef stock
Salt and freshly ground black pepper

Prepare bouquet garni by wrapping parsley, celery, thyme, peppercorns and bay leaf inside a piece of cheesecloth and tying it with kitchen string.

In a medium saucepan over high heat, melt butter. Add onions, carrots and celery and sauté for 15 minutes until vegetables are turning golden brown.

Reduce heat to low and add flour, stirring continuously until flour turns brown. Add tomato paste and cook for another 2 minutes.

Gradually whisk in stock, add the bouquet garni and adjust seasoning with salt and pepper. Bring to a boil, regularly skimming off froth that rises to the surface. Simmer for about 45 minutes, until the sauce has reduced by half.

Strain through a fine sieve lined with several layers of cheesecloth.

Use immediately or freeze it in small containers and use as needed.

Makes 2 cups (500 ml).

Demi-Glace

1 cup (250 ml) brown sauce
1 cup (250 ml) beef stock
Salt and freshly ground black pepper

In a medium saucepan over medium heat, combine the stocks and simmer for about 30 minutes, until reduced by half.

Strain through a fine sieve lined with several layers of cheesecloth. Adjust seasoning with salt and pepper.

Use demi-glace immediately or freeze it in small containers and use as needed.

Makes 1 cup (250 ml).

Simple Syrup

1/4 cup (60 g) granulated sugar
1/4 cup (60 ml) water

Prepare syrup by mixing all ingredients in a small saucepan and boiling until sugar is melted, or about 5 minutes. Remove from heat and allow cooling. Transfer into a glass bottle and refrigerate. Simple syrup will keep for 2 to 3 weeks in the refrigerator.

Cooking Terms

AL DENTE: Italian for "to the tooth" and is used to describe a food that is cooked until it gives a slight resistance when one bites into it.

BLANCHING: Cooking a food very briefly and partially in boiling water or hot fat as part of a combination cooking method. Usually used to loosen peels from vegetables and fruits.

BLENDING: A mixing method in which two or more ingredients are combined until they are evenly distributed; a spoon, rubber spatula, whisk or electric mixer with its paddle attachment can be used.

BOIL: To cook in water or other liquid at an approximate temperature of 212°F or 100°C at sea level.

BROIL: To cook by heat radiating from an overhead source.

BOUQUET GARNI: A blend of herbs and vegetables tied in a bundle with twine and used to flavor stocks, soups, sauces and stews.

CARAMELIZE: Fruits and vegetables with natural sugars can be caramelized by sautéing, roasting or grilling, giving them a sweet flavor and golden glaze.

CHIFFONADE: To slice into thin strips or shreds.

CLARIFIED BUTTER: Purified butterfat; the butter is melted and water and milk solids are removed; also known as drawn butter.

CONCASSÉ: To chop coarsely.

DEGLAZE: To swirl or stir a liquid like wine or stock in a pan to dissolve cooked food particles remaining on the bottom, using the mixture as the base for the sauce.

DEGREASE: To skim the fat from the top of a liquid.

DICE: To cut food into cubes.

DREDGE: To coat food with flour, breadcrumbs or cornmeal before frying.

FLAMBÉ: Pour warmed spirits such as brandy, whisky or rum over foods such as fruits or meat and then ignite it.

FOLD: To combine a light ingredient like egg whites with a much heavier mixture like whipped cream.

FRY: To cook in hot fat.

GELATIN: A colorless, odorless and flavorless mixture of proteins made from animal bones, connective tissues and certain algae; when dissolved in warm liquid it forms a jelly-like substance used as a thickener for desserts, cold soups and certain sauces.

GRILL: Cooking in which the heat source is located beneath the rack on which the food is placed.

JULIENNE: Foods cut into matchstick shapes.

MACERATE: Soaking fruits in liquid, such as brandy or other alcoholic ingredients, so they absorb that flavor. Macerate can also be fruits sprinkled with sugar, which draws out the natural juices of the fruit, creating a syrup.

MARINADE: A seasoned liquid in which raw foods are soaked or coated to absorb flavors and/or become tender before cooking.

MINCE: To cut or chop a food finely.

MONTER: To finish a sauce by swirling or whisking in butter until it is melted.

PAN-BROIL: To cook food uncovered and without fat.

PAN-FRY: To cook food in a moderate amount of hot fat, uncovered.

POACH: To gently cook food submerged in a simmering liquid.

PURÉE: To process food to achieve a smooth pulp.

REDUCE: To cook by simmering a liquid until the quantity decreases by evaporation.

REFRESH: The process of submerging food (usually vegetables) in cold water to cool it quickly and prevent further cooking.

SEAR: To brown a food quickly over high heat.

SEASON: Adding flavor to foods. Season can also mean to coat the surface of a new pot or pan with vegetable oil and place in a hot oven for about 1 hour. As the oil burns off, the carbon residue fills in the small pits and groves of the pan's surface making a smooth finish that helps prevent food from sticking.

SIMMER: To maintain the temperature of a liquid just below the boiling point.

STIR-FRY: To cook food over high heat with little fat while stirring constantly and briskly.

Index

This cookbook is the reflection of the ongoing commitment and relentless pursuit of Royal Caribbean International Culinary, Beverage and Restaurant Operation teams to quality and innovation.

The creation of *Carte du Jour* would not have been possible without the support of:

Richard Fain, Chairman and CEO of Royal Caribbean Cruises, Ltd;
Adam Goldstein, President and CEO of Royal Caribbean International and
Lisa Bauer, SR. VP Hotel Operations of Royal Caribbean International.

Additional Appreciation to:
Josef Jungwirth, Director of Fleet Culinary Operations,
Bob Midyette, Director of Fleet Beverage Operations,
Ken Taylor, Director of Fleet Restaurant Operations,
Naomi Celaire-Hattema, Traveling Beverage Manager,
Marco Marama, Senior Executive Chef,
Robert Mead, Corporate Pastry Chef,
Travis Kamiyama, Chef Consultant Izumi,
Keriann Von Raestfeld, Chef de Cuisine Consultant, 150 Central Park and
Corinne Lewis, Manager, Catering & Retail Operations and cookbook author.

Special thanks to photographer Matthew Pace, and
Tad Ware & Company Publishing and Photography team for their creativity.